Design and Truth

DESIGN AND TRUTH

ROBERT GRUDIN

Yale
UNIVERSITY PRESS

New Haven and London

Designed by Nancy Ovedovitz and set in Adobe Garamond and
HFJ Gotham type by Duke & Company, Devon, Pennsylvania.
Printed in the United States of America by Sheridan Books,
Ann Arbor, Michigan.

Library of Congress Cataloging-in-Publication Data
Grudin, Robert.
Design and truth / Robert Grudin.
p. cm.
Includes bibliographical references and index.
ISBN 978-0-300-16140-3 (alk. paper)
1. Design. 2. Truth. I. Title.
NK1505.G75 2010
745.401—dc22   2009041254

A catalogue record for this book is available from
the British Library.

This paper meets the requirements of ANSI/NISO Z39.48-1992
(Permanence of Paper).

10 9 8 7 6 5 4 3 2 1

Lisa Taylor, in memoriam
Bill Stumpf, in memoriam
Clark Malcolm

For their civility

Contents

ONE

HOMAGE TO RIKYU: DESIGN, TRUTH, AND POWER

1 Sen no Rikyu and the Paradox of Innovation 3

2 Good Design Tells the Truth 10

3 What Design and Truth Say about Each Other 27

4 Design as Tragedy: The Rise and Fall of the Twin Towers 34

5 Edsel's Law: How Bad Design Happens 46

6 Designs of Darkness 55

7 Face to Face with Design 62

TWO

HOMAGE TO VASARI: DESIGN, KNOWLEDGE, AND ENERGY

8 Giorgio Vasari and the Permutations of Design 85

9 The Lady in the Picture: Design and Revelation
in Renaissance Art 88

CONTENTS

10   In Jefferson's Footsteps: Modes of Self-Design   105

11   Jefferson's Gravestone: Metaphorical Extensions
     of Design   117

12   Liberty as a Knowledge Design   134

13   Corporate Redesign and the Business of Knowledge   150

14   Designing Time   166

15   The Design of Private Knowledge   178

Epilogue: Designing Truth   193

Notes   197

Acknowledgments   211

Index   213

Color plates follow page 40

HOMAGE TO RIKYU:
DESIGN, TRUTH, AND POWER

Sen no Rikyu and the Paradox of Innovation

Everyone designs who devises courses of action aimed at changing
existing situations into preferred ones. The intellectual activity that
produces material artifacts is no different fundamentally from the one
that prescribes remedies for a sick patient or the one that devises a
new sales plan for a company or a social welfare policy for a state.

HERBERT SIMON

After the sixteenth-century warlord Toyotomi Hideyoshi had established control over the bulk of Japan, he asked the celebrated
Sen no Rikyu to join his court at Seikenji. Rikyu (1522–91) was the
acknowledged master of the Japanese tea ceremony. He was already
known as a great man and had received honors that even an emperor might envy. Rikyu accepted the invitation but did not show
up at Hideyoshi's palace at the expected hour. Hideyoshi waited and
waited. What could be keeping the man?

When Rikyu finally appeared, Hideyoshi testily asked what had
made him so late. Rikyu answered that he had been drinking tea.
This unceremonious response was too much for the peeved warlord.
He grabbed a bamboo tea ladle that Rikyu had brought with him
and snapped it in half. For Rikyu that ladle had been an icon. A

present from his favorite teacher, it symbolized to him the understated eloquence of design that was known as *wabi-cha*. For Hideyoshi, the ladle symbolized something else: the puniness of a subject who needed a lesson in manners.

The rift between the two men soon widened. Rikyu's commitment to creating, in the tea ceremony, a culture of simplicity, equality, and integrity clashed with Hideyoshi's passion for a ceremony rich in the accoutrements of power: ornament, display, and social inequality. Rikyu's fame and influence, moreover, threatened Hideyoshi's confidence. One day in the spring of 1591, the autocrat demanded that the designer commit suicide. Rikyu had no choice but to obey.[1]

Design is the purest exercise of human skill. To add a new instrument or process to the design treasury is to engage in the force of evolving nature. Each new design is a new discovery, conveying a specific truth about our relationship to nature and to each other. Rikyu's designs exerted enormous influence after his death. By redesigning the tea ceremony, he created a social avenue of truth: an interpersonal medium where the exchange of useful knowledge could proceed simply and lucidly, without interference from extraneous influences like social rank. Rikyu expressed the meaning of this knowledge-based innovation in a haiku:

Sometimes a person may feel embarrassed to ask questions.
That embarrassment should be set aside and questions asked.

Rikyu's reform of the tea ceremony established a cultural matrix that would bring his nation into the modern world. But unfortunately his creative power did not translate into immediate political pull. For all his greatness of spirit, he was at the mercy of a jealous warlord. He could not, except perhaps by martyrdom, engrave his message onto the face of the world around him.[2] The same irony applies to almost all designers. However grand their aspirations, they wait upon the will of people in power. And power, which can ratify the truth of good design, can, conversely, debase design into a fabric of lies.

Rikyu's story raises a number of questions about the nature and scope of design: How does it relate to its political and economic context? Is it a specialized pursuit or does it function in all of our lives? To what extent can human interactions be designed along creative principles? Are our lives subject to the designs of others? If so, can we design a way to our own liberation?

To address these issues, we must first appreciate the role of design in the context—or contexts—of human experience.

We can start off with a working definition of what design does.

Design shapes, regulates, and channels energy, empowering forces that might otherwise be spent chaotically. In the design of a house, the energy to be shaped and channeled is that of the air and light that run through the halls and windows and rooms, and of the people who dwell there. In the design of a car, the energy is the power train and the passengers. In the design of a formula or a work of art, the energy is meaning.

Designs have meanings of their own, too. Every realized design is a module of embodied knowledge, and much of this knowledge is readily translatable into words. Dress designs and car designs are seen as making "statements"; regional architectural styles are often called "vernacular." These meanings can intensify or suppress the energy that design shapes and channels. Design can sing out the essence of energy, as with the Jaguar XKE (1961–68), or ignore this essence in an exploitive quest for mass-market appeal, as with the Ford Edsel (1958–60). Such variations occur because design mediates between creativity and economics. The energy field created by a given design is situated in the larger energy field that is the marketplace.

Design's location in the marketplace gives it a profoundly moral character. At one end of the ethical spectrum, design can be a muse; at the other, a prostitute. We have already considered the tragic example of Rikyu. In this book we will consider other extremes, too:

In 1525, Federico Gonzaga, ruler of Mantua, instructed the artist Giulio Romano to build and decorate a palace just outside town on a marsh called Te. Federico allowed Giulio's extravagant imagination free play. Giulio and his men labored for eight years. In the end they produced an astonishing work of art, a palace full of variety and surprises but true to a singular esthetic idea. Giulio's work remains a tribute to Renaissance imagination and vision.

In 1962 the New York City Port Authority hired the architect Minoru Yamasaki to build a world trade center. After elaborate research and review, Yamasaki presented a proposal for a large architectural complex that would gracefully complement the existing skyline of Lower Manhattan. The Port Authority trashed this proposal and demanded something more massive. Yamasaki complied, and the result was a twinned colossus that insulted the skyline, posed safety hazards, and offended fundamentalist Islamists. In 2001, with catastrophic loss of life, his work was destroyed by a group of fanatics.

Design waits on its political milieu. In an enlightened marketplace, good design reigns paramount; in a debased marketplace, design is either dismissed entirely or rudely contorted, sometimes into monstrous form.

But the marketplace, indeed politics itself, is subject to design. Legal and cultural paradigms are not normally spoken of as designs, but in fact they are blueprints that sculpt the character of large populations and channel human energies in specific directions. The US Constitution is the design equivalent of the Jaguar XKE and the Palazzo Te: it liberates human energies and maximizes human options. The culture under Hideyoshi was like the Ford Edsel: it trapped the human will in ungainly applications and monolithic paradigms. Something similar can be said about works of art and literature, as well as about the various designs of corporations and foundations. To a significant extent, it is these embodied or enacted concepts—call them *knowledge designs*—that inspire or suppress the energies of a given culture.

Overarching even these are the energies and designs of nature, so magnificent that billions of people still believe them to be the work of a Great Designer. Although overwhelming evidence speaks against this theory, the cosmic order is so dazzling that it inspires reverence in and of itself. In its enormous variety and incessant bursts of genius, nature has inspired countless human designers. Nature, moreover, tests our own designs and often files a boisterous complaint when they are not up to speed.

It is the psychological and moral power of design, however, that will concern me most here. For all its potential sophistication, there is something primal and essential about the act of designing, as though, more than any other act, it brings us in touch with our own nature. Design is so fundamentally human that our species has been called *Homo faber* (man the maker), implying that no historical influence will ever alienate us from the meticulous process of refitting our world. Design is a primary medium of human liberty, too: we must either design our own lives or subject ourselves to the designs of others.

The practice of design, however humble its objectives, can be liberating and renewing. My own simple design of a repair kit for broken television remotes, and the way this design liberated me from helpless anger, will serve as an example of the healing power of design in a world of perplexed and frustrated consumers. More seriously, we will visit the achievement of Baldassare Castiglione, who designed a social medium that brought his nation away from feudal society and into the modern world; the testimony of Giorgio Vasari, who gave us the first modern theory of design; and the life and work of Thomas Jefferson, who brought a designer's perspective to much of what he touched. These examples and others will speak to the value of design as a functioning attitude, a modus operandi that allows individuals to engage life meaningfully and to readdress personal and professional issues with a new sense of freedom. My broader purpose in this study is to wrest design from the possessive grip of corporations and to return it, insofar as possible, to the hands of the individual.

There is, finally, the relationship between design and truth. Because our designs convey solid meaning, and because they interface between us and the world, they must tell us the truth about the world and tell the world the truth about us. A well-designed hoe speaks the truth to the ground that it breaks and, conversely, tells us the truth about the ground. The same can be said about any product of invention, be it mechanical, like a car, or intellectual, like a speech. Good design enables honest and effective engagement with the world. Poor design is symptomatic either of inadequate insight or of a fraudulent and exploitive strategy of production. If good design tells the truth, poor design tells a lie, a lie usually related, in one way or another, to the getting or abusing of power.

My extended essay has two parts. In Part One ("Homage to Rikyu: Design, Truth, and Power") I will dwell on design under the stresses of the real-world marketplace and will test the premise that "good design tells the truth." In Part Two ("Homage to Vasari: Design, Knowledge, and Energy") I will explore the effects of design on psychological and social dynamics by testing the relevance of design principles in areas of human activity where they are not normally applied. Beginning with the psychology of art and ranging more and more freely, these meditations will conclude with a discussion of what is perhaps the most intimate aspect of design, the ways, both conscious and unconscious, in which we design our mental worlds.

2

Good Design Tells the Truth

Compare two views, each expressed by a famous modern designer:

To drink water from a waxed paper cup on the highway and to drink it from a crystal goblet are different gestures. In the first case, you almost forget that you exist as you drink. In the second . . . you realize that you have in your hands an instrument that makes you reflect upon how you are living at that moment.[1]

Probably the most widely recognized of all the Eames furniture designs, the Eames lounge chair occupies a favored place in thousands of living rooms, studies, libraries, and dens—as well as in the permanent collection of New York's Museum of Modern Art. Charles Eames's aspirations for the chair were less lofty. He wanted it to have "the warm receptive look of a well used first baseman's mitt."[2]

These two views represent polarities in the theory and practice of design. For Ettore Sottsass, design must make a statement that lends excitement and dignity to an implement's use. For Charles Eames, a design is defined and dignified by use itself. Sottsass privileges form over function; Eames implies that expressed functionality is the purest sort of form. Although the form-function issue may seem academic, its applications can produce dramatic consequences, especially when the design involved is an expression of public policy.

Designs Collide in Paris

One balmy summer night in Paris many years ago, I motorcycled with a passenger through the short tunnel in the north wing of the Palais du Louvre and onto the Place du Carrousel. I was in the fast lane, doing about thirty miles per hour. I leaned into a left turn and instantaneously got a close-up view of the rear end of a car that had stopped dead in my lane. There was no time to swerve, brake, or pray.

I was lucky. As the bike slammed into the car, the handlebar absorbed much of the impact, twisting grotesquely in my hands and slowing my forward motion enough to prevent fractures. I was doubly fortunate in that the light metal of the car bent as my knees and knuckles hit it.

Another design feature of the car turned out luckily as well. My passenger, Jim Breasted, had taken flight, hurtling over my back, rolling over the roof of the car, and subsiding on the pavement in front. A competition skier, he knew how to take falls. He was momentarily dazed but otherwise unhurt. The car's fabric roof, light metal, and rounded front-to-back design had cushioned his descent.

These results were all accidental: felicitous contacts in what could have been a nasty wreck. But a third surprising result was no accident at all. The car was totaled. My front wheel had penetrated to the car's frame and bent it irreparably, then bounced back without so much as a flat tire.

Why was this no accident? Consider the two vehicles. The motorcycle was a 1956 Norton Dominator 99, prince of British bikes. It was solidly built and finely balanced. Its aerodynamic design whispered

Howard Rower astride the author's Norton Dominator.
St. Gotthard Pass, Switzerland, summer 1960. Photograph by author.

of a clear day, an empty road, and the rush of air. The Dominator had made such a splash in the world of design that French president Charles de Gaulle had ordered at least a dozen of them for his guard of honor. The car was a Citroën Deux Chevaux, the French equivalent of a Volkswagen bug, but so ungainly that it made the bug look like a Lotus by comparison. The Deux Chevaux was built of light components for marketability and economy. Performance, comfort, beauty, and security were not its design priorities. The Deux Chevaux had never been crash-tested; it just looked that way.[3]

The violent encounter of Dominator with Deux Chevaux was thus a symbolic meeting between two primary players in the form-function dynamic that characterizes all design. The Deux Chevaux exemplified the hegemony of function over form: the subordination of all design priorities to the idea of cheap and trusty transportation. Other instances of emphatic functionality include Levittown and other low-priced housing developments, military and other institutional technologies, and most hand tools. The Norton, on the other hand, was a marriage of form and function: a synthesis in which graceful design suggested superb functionality and in fact contributed to it. Other examples of this happy blend include the Toyota Prius, the Taconic State Parkway, the original Casio G-Shock wristwatch, and, last but not least, the Parisian baguette.

But what of the missing extreme, the tyranny of form over function? To find a good example of this, we may look to the oft-cited but still helpful example of the Ford Edsel. In 1958 the Ford Motor Company had introduced the Edsel to compete for a share of the market between its mid-priced Mercury and its high-priced Lincoln. What motivated the Edsel's design was Ford's perceived need to make a big splash that would improve sales. Ford might have done so successfully by stealing a page from the book of European manufacturers who made comfortable cars that performed ably. Instead, Ford decided to test the limits of Detroit's penchant for mass-market battleships.

The Edsel, as one source put it, came in two sizes, "big and bigger." The larger version weighed more than two tons, much of which was made up by its giant body, which seemed to hang loosely on a more compact frame: from the side, the car looked like an ersatz space vehicle. Its rear end was dominated by gull wing brake lights so huge that they parodied their own usefulness. The front end resembled a female body part, with headlights.

The design of the Edsel, like that of so many American cars of its time, sent two distinct messages. The first message was that in the fantasy world of Hollywood, *I Love Lucy,* and *Your Hit Parade,* function is irrelevant. Roads were made to be tamed, not felt, and driving should feel as little like driving as possible (the car came with optional push-button gears). The second message was that the American consumer's idea of formal beauty was less an image of relevance to life as lived than an adolescent dream of material excess and arrogant power: you will never be able to afford a palace, but you can drive around in one. Messages of this sort kept the pots boiling in Detroit for decades.

But people both inside and outside Ford apparently felt that it had pushed the design envelope too far. Ford vice president Robert McNamara had no great love for the Edsel division and offered little support. Sales were never robust, and by 1959 dealers themselves were opting out. Ford sold its last Edsel in 1960, the year the Norton Dominator met the Deux Chevaux.[4]

Deux Chevaux, Dominator, Edsel. Of these three designs, Edsel should concern us most seriously. The Deux Chevaux effects are easy enough to understand; they can be linked to basic economic survival strategies. The Dominator effects, theoretically considered, go at least as far back as the days of the architect Louis Sullivan, who wrote in 1896 that form follows function.[5] This principle has become intrinsic to the study of design. But the Edsel, complete with its anatomically suggestive grille, sits sphinxlike and unexamined. Why do people overdesign when good design is cheaper to build, cheaper to buy, and more sustainable? Let us begin with two simple working hypotheses:

If design is itself a medium of social interactions, overdesign
    is a symptom of interactions that are dysfunctional.
And if, as is generally acknowledged, design is a kind of rheto-

ric, overdesign is an opportunistic abuse of rhetoric in the application of some form of power.

The Edsel offers substantial support for these hypotheses. During the mid-1950s, when it was under development, cars and drivers loomed even larger in the American economy than they do in the early twenty-first century. Advertising campaigns and a barrage of creature comforts had convinced most American consumers that big was beautiful, and the production of large money-eating, gas-guzzling cars was turning handsome profits. Detroit overdesigned because overdesign was a cash cow. True, the Edsel was a bridge too far, but even so, its existence points to the corporate greed that flaunted safety, sound engineering, economy, beauty, and good taste during Detroit's era of hegemony in the American car market. Although the Edsel was anything but a fictional vehicle, it was nonetheless an example of fictive marketing: a quest for sales based on an inflation and distortion of the national sense of self. This mind-set has never gone away: by 2009 it had driven two of Detroit's three remaining auto companies into bankruptcy.

Overdesign and Public Policy

Examples of architectural overdesign suggest interesting parallels to the Edsel. The first is from Renaissance Rome and concerns the construction of the present St. Peter's Basilica. Popes and architects had spent decades debating the design of the church, drawing and redrawing plans. Michelangelo, who took charge of the project in 1546, chose to adapt a design that had been submitted years before by the brilliant Donato Bramante (1444–1514). The plan called for a massive dome set atop a perfectly symmetrical building in the shape

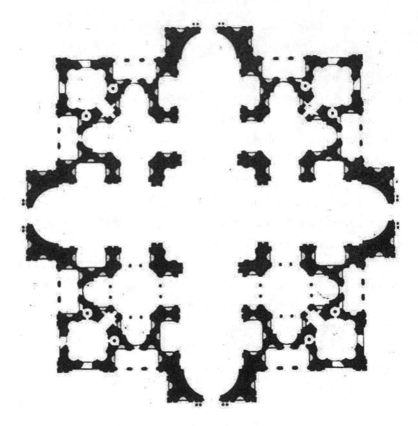

Donato Bramante's plan for St. Peter's Basilica.

of a Greek cross. In 1564, Michelangelo died with the church still under construction; and although his replacement, Giacomo della Porta, labored to realize his plan, papal policy changed. Pope Paul V (reigned 1605–21) decided to build the world's biggest church in order to advertise Rome's hegemony and papal power. In 1606 he commissioned Carlo Maderno to add on the long nave that now faces the Piazza San Pietro. By the time of the basilica's dedication in 1626, Bramante and Michelangelo's unique and graceful design had been expanded to

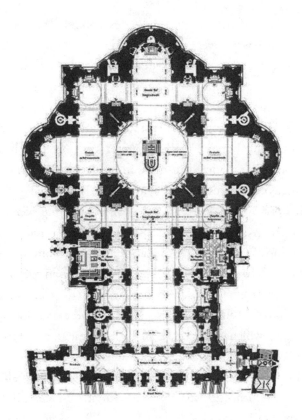

Carlo Maderno's plan for St. Peter's Basilica.

make a baroque barn whose sole symbolic purpose was to proclaim the centralized and overwhelming power of Rome and the pope.[6]

The story of St. Peter's suggests that when form is privileged emphatically enough, it can achieve a perverse functionality of its own. Here a church, nominally a place of worship, became an engine of temporal power. This idea of design as power was not lost on the Nazi architect Albert Speer (1905–81), who visited St. Peter's shortly before embarking on what would have been his own most massive project, the Berlin Hall of the People (Halle des Volkes). This neo-Roman building, which was never completed and exists now only as a model, would have contained a room large enough to hold four St. Peter's Basilicas, with space to spare. Its dome, rising more than a thousand feet, would have been topped by a lantern that was itself the size of St. Peter's dome. Adolf Hitler (himself an artist fond of architectural studies) enthusiastically collaborated in the design process. After all, how could absolute power be rendered in more intimidating fashion than by a mountainous construction in the symbolic garb of ancient Rome? Hitler's only worry was that Stalin might build something even bigger.[7]

Which brings us back to Ettore Sottsass and Charles Eames. Sottsass is in the camp of Pope Paul V, Albert Speer, and the Ford Motor Company. In characterizing form (the "crystal goblet") as an overwhelming, even existential element of design, he was, willy-nilly, buying into the rhetoric of power. Thus he put himself firmly in the tradition of "decorative" design, which in its most extreme manifestation (the sword and the shield only for show, the vases that hold nothing, the "show kitchens" built not to be used) is form without any function at all. Eames had a different form-function relation in mind, one along the lines of the Norton Dominator. In giving his chair "the warm receptive look of a well used first baseman's mitt," he implied that form should be the honest advertisement of function—in fact, the communicative dimension of use itself. This does not mean that Eames had no regard for beauty. He simply understood that beauty in its highest expression develops as a statement of, or response to, the operations of nature.[8]

Design as Cultural Hijacking: Pei, Serra, Christo, Gehry

In the Edsel, St. Peter's Basilica, and Speer's Hall of the People, we have seen three instances of overdesign as a rhetoric of corporate or institutional power. Now let us turn to four designers who redefined public space in a way that belied its customary intention and instead drew attention to their own art.

A stranger walking into I. M. Pei's addition to the National Gallery of Art in Washington, DC, might well ask, "Very impressive, but who stole the collection?" The perplexing answer to this question is that Pei stole it himself, if only figuratively. His soaring design for the interior is so visually intrusive that it steals our attention from the relatively small collection of artworks inside it. How can we characterize Pei's architectural performance? Here the language of architecture proves less useful to us than the language of oratory. Designing a public building is, in effect, conveying a public message. In this case the message of Pei's building—that museums are built to preserve art—is drowned out by the rhetoric.

Unless, of course, the rhetoric is the message itself. Was Pei, late in life, designing his own personal monument? Was he implying the superiority of architecture to any art it might contain? In either case, or both, he has left us an image of form overreaching function.

Overreaching was stretched further by Richard Serra, whose 120-foot-long *Tilted Arc* was installed in Federal Plaza, New York City, in 1981. The low, plain structure all but destroyed the plaza as a pedestrian right-of-way, as was apparently Serra's implicit purpose in designing it. What but a prohibitively encroaching sculptural barrier could fully drive home the idea of the artist's empowerment over the masses? Apparently unconvinced by this statement, the public let out a cry of pain that lasted until the *Arc* was torn down in 1989, the same year that saw the demise of the Berlin Wall.

Consider now a less daunting example of artist-driven overdesign, Christo (and Jeanne-Claude)'s installation of gates in Central Park, New York City, in 2005. Christo, a Bulgarian artist who discovered long ago that most public art is little more than a massive multiplication of banalities, apparently decided to exploit this fact with humor and Dadaist bravado. Representing himself as an avant-garde minimalist, he embarked on a series of extensive installations that repackaged public space. His operative principle, reminiscent of the literary theories of Jacques Derrida, is that art can deconstruct mental space, thereby changing the beholders' image of their own existential location. But Christo's gates, like his other famous multiplications, are void of essential significance, leading only to each other. The rhetoric of *The Gates* is empty. The message would seem to be that space is meaningless, except in affording an artist the means for self-advertisement.

When we are faced with such aggressive and disingenuous assertions of design, approved by committees and laid as faits accomplis upon the communal doorstep, we sometimes can do little more than articulate our pain.[9] Alternatively we can convert such artsy pyrotechnics into objects of criticism or butts of satire.[10] But these are essentially futile gestures, minor mishaps in the day of the cheerful monster that is Public Art. Occasionally, however, overdesign pushes so far beyond the form-function equilibrium that it runs afoul of the laws of nature. In such cases, retribution is swift and, refreshingly, public. This is what befell the clever but chronically overdesigning architect Frank Gehry, as reported in the *New York Times:*

> The Massachusetts Institute of Technology has sued the architect Frank Gehry and a construction company, claiming that "design and construction failures" in the institute's $300 million Stata Center resulted in pervasive leaks, cracks and drainage problems that have required costly repairs.
>
> The center, which features angular sections that appear to be falling on top of one another, opened to great acclaim in the

spring of 2004. Mr. Gehry once said that it "looks like a party of drunken robots got together to celebrate."[11]

Mr. Gehry, in his own defense, might claim that his architectural opus was only doing its postmodern job: that it had not only seemed to be falling apart but eventually succeeded in doing exactly that.

Good Design Tells the Truth

Readers may not agree with all of my conclusions about Paul V, Pei, Serra, Christo, or Gehry, but our evidence nonetheless suggests that the Edsel hypothesis seems to work: When overdesign occurs, it signals some public boondoggle.

And if the Edsel hypothesis did *not* work, there would be cause for alarm. In treating design as a form of rhetoric, we must agree that it falls under the classic laws of rhetorical interaction. These interactions inhere in all social phenomena, including commerce, politics, war, religion, and love. Even body language is a form of rhetoric. In all of these interactions, an excess of rhetorical zeal is usually the first sign of manipulation and deception. Mass-market advertising, campaign speeches, jingoism, evangelistic tirades, and seductive crooning all display the same link between exaggerated rhetoric and attempted exploitation. Indeed, we are so deep in spin that we sometimes forget that there is such a thing as truth and that people exist who are ready to tell it.

Perhaps the best lesson we can learn from the Deux Chevaux, the Norton, and the Edsel is this: good design tells the truth. What it promises is what it unequivocally delivers. My Norton motorcycle told the truth with its solid feel and graceful lines; it delivered the truth when it saved me from serious injury that summer night in Paris. The Norton proved without question that its design was not just about pleasure and power and beauty but also about the well-being of its driver.

I sit at the keyboard of a computer designed in part by Jef Raskin, who compared good designers to good physicians. My office chair was co-designed by Bill Stumpf, who saw good design as part of a generalized civility that could renew the world. Behind it, facing the north windows of my study, is the lounge chair designed by Charles Eames. Raskin, Stumpf, and Eames are all famous for their original minds. But they could not have achieved originality if they had not approached their tasks with simple candor. Good designers are truth-tellers, facilitators in the dialogue that allows us to comprehend and engage reality.

If good design tells us the truth, it seems fair to ask what that truth is. One might respond casually that each design carries its own distinct message or set of messages: well-designed cars tell us the truth about driving, roads, destinations; well-designed houses speak truly of many matters relating to private and communal space. These honesties can affect us deeply and permanently. Here is the novelist John Galsworthy remembering his childhood response to the sight of well-made foot-wear: "They were too beautiful—the pair of pumps, so inexpressibly slim, the patent leathers with cloth tops, making water come into one's mouth, the tall brown riding boots with marvelous sooty glow, as if, though new, they had been worn a hundred years. Those pairs could only have been made by one who saw before him the Soul of Boot—so truly were they prototypes incarnating the very spirit of all foot-gear."[12] Smitten with awe and something akin to love, the boy was for-ever altered. He developed not only a respect for art but a benchmark of quality against which to judge all things. Galsworthy might have titled his memoir "Gessler's Boots." Instead he called it "Quality."

A similar idea pops up at the opening of Raymond Chandler's

masterpiece, *The Long Goodbye:* "The first time I laid eyes on Terry Lennox he was drunk in a Rolls-Royce Silver Wraith outside the terrace of The Dancers. The parking lot attendant had brought the car out and he was still holding the door open because Terry Lennox's left foot was still dangling outside, as if he had forgotten he had one. . . . There was a girl beside him. Her hair was a lovely shade of dark red and she had a distant smile on her lips and over her shoulders she had a blue mink that almost made the Rolls-Royce look like just another automobile. It didn't quite. Nothing can."[13] For Chandler the Rolls-Royce is an image of quality in human interactions, of the honesty, integrity, and fidelity that will be tested in all the major characters in the novel.

From Galsworthy and Chandler we may infer that good design speaks to us, not just in particulars but in more general truths as well. In a world where technology dominates our interface with reality, good design ensures that this interface is effective and personal and complete. As John Heskett says, a well-designed artifact (in his case, a knife) is "an extension of the senses."[14] Good design allows for an honest dialogue with the world at large. Good design tells us that although the world is challenging and dangerous, there are solid means of engaging it. And beyond this, good design speaks to us of the quality and joy of the engagement.

An example of this truth and eloquence in action is the Polynesian pole house, found throughout the Pacific tropics. Twenty or so heavy poles are set in the ground, and the house is built on them. Windows and doors are numerous and large, making the house a shrine of sorts to the earth's two ranking deities, light and air. Every room has at least one doorway opening broadly to a garden or a deck. The roof overhangs generously to protect from heat and rain. The cathedral ceilings are vented to allow hot air to escape. The house offers security yet invites activity. It spaciously welcomes human use yet extends itself into nature. It achieves human richness without show or expense. Its high ceilings radiate freedom and conjure up daydreams, memories, and aspirations. It speaks to us of what we are and what we want to be.

This attitude toward design is brought home by an anecdote told by Matt Taylor, a student of Frank Lloyd Wright's, about "Usonians," the affordable houses that Wright was building.

> During my time at Taliesin, I was able to talk to many owners of Usonians. They talked about their environments with unreserved passion. It was from one, Mrs. Pew, that I learned the true secret of Mr. Wright's genius and success. She described how at first she hated the house. She felt that Mr. Wright had not listened to her requirements but merely built what he wanted. She was, at the end of her second year living in it, ready to sell it and move on—at great financial sacrifice. She told me that she decided that she would "give the house another year without struggling with it" before she made up her mind. In that year, a transformation took place. She discovered that "Mr. Wright had not built a house for who I was"—but for "the person that I could become. It turned out that Mr. Wright had listened well and understood me very deeply."[15]

Good design is the material image of mental health. Design can reintegrate our character and fulfill our awareness. We follow good design to discover what is good in ourselves.

Another word about my faithful Norton Dominator 99. Designed by Bert Hopwood and built at Norton's Bracebridge Street works in Birmingham, England, the model remained current for several years; then it was replaced by the heftier Atlas, which itself gave way to the even higher-powered Commando. But what these later models gained in power, they lost in good manners. I have ridden several other well-known bikes, including the legendary Vincent, but none of them came close to the Dominator's package of lightness, balance, and verve. I remember days of sun-drenched, windswept rapture as I toured alone on the country roads of France and England, the secluded villages, the pleasant stops and chats with ever-curious townspeople, the remarkable communion with the machine. One of the many signs of its sweetness was the day I carried a young British hitchhiker all the way from the Channel into London and turned around to find her fast asleep. The Dominator projected my excitement abroad, to bemused elders and to new friends, to fellow students in Dublin and to total strangers in Wales, who, after an evening of beer and song, carried me onto the Dublin ferry. The Dominator, which had already told me all about Europe, told me as well that finely built machines can reflect and amplify our humanity.

Such are the truths that design can convey. Overdesign, conversely, is a pack of lies. With the Edsel and its ilk, Detroit deceived Americans into believing that personal success and dignity were available only through arrogant display, environmental waste, pollution, flawed safeguards, and poor performance. Pope Paul V, who threw out the original Bramante-Michelangelo design for St. Peter's Basilica, simply because he wanted to build the world's biggest church, spawned the colossal lie that bigger is better for religion, as someday it would be for motorcars. These lies of overdesign are not isolated lies; rather, they are symbolic of what has become ubiquitous. Even the processed food on our supermarket shelves lies to our bodies by pandering to our cravings rather than nourishing us.[16] Overdesign will always lie because it will always spring from a corrupt relationship between producer and consumer.

I should finish the Paris story. The Deux Chevaux in question was occupied by a young Parisian couple who had (as they later confessed to me) paused momentarily on the road to discuss whether or not to go to the opera. After the collision the young woman rushed from the car and found Jim Breasted in front of it, lying on his back. She sat down and cradled his head in her lap, and he awoke to see her face quite beautifully outlined against the stars. Soon the Paris police arrived, accompanied by an ambulance. Two officials stuffed the Norton into the ambulance, where it fit rather snugly, and drove off with it to points unknown. The others jailed me for driving without my passport. On my release I made for London. After a week's recuperation at the home of a friend, I was ready to make more mischief. I returned to Paris, reclaimed my victorious Dominator, and headed for my digs in Dublin. The bike drove perfectly, although its bent-down handlebars forced me into a kind of racing posture.

Jim Breasted lives near Aspen, where he still skis competitively and has been known to attend one of that town's annual celebrations, the International Design Conference.

3

What Design and Truth Say about Each Other

What is truth? For our purposes here, a simple answer will suffice: Truth is the laws of nature as we experience them on Earth. Truth determines that our bodies do not take off into the air and float about like birthday balloons. Truth asserts, without fear of contradiction, that light of a certain spectrum makes things visible, that pleasure is sweet and pain is a drag. We may sit in a seminar and debate the nature of truth ad nauseam. But the truth lies in the rough but workable details of what we are and where we are.

How, then, does good design tell the truth? By framing appropriate responses to the truths that nature tells us. Hunters and gatherers designed, farmers and herders designed, villagers and townspeople designed. Over time, the poorer designs generally vanished, while the better designs stuck. Designers spoke to nature and listened to nature's response. Good design emerged as an apt response to truth. Design mimicked and emulated natural truth by being true to nature.

I must add, however, that design is inherently self-proliferating. We cannot recognize, within ourselves, a degree of control over nature without the desire to multiply that power, to move beyond existing boundaries, to achieve unheard-of security and freedom. Human designs—thriving towns, good roads, mathematical arts, efficient machines, precise language—function simultaneously as goods to be enjoyed and platforms for further achievement. In the years since the advent of printing in Europe in 1450, the rate of progress has increased exponentially, culminating in a century that began with people groveling about on Earth and ended with their putting a communicative robot on Mars. Design has established itself as a kind of nature-in-nature, an arbiter of time and space.

Which brings us to the rub. Thanks to growth and proliferation in design itself, design is no longer in intimate and exclusive dialogue with nature, or with nature's truth. Now the mix is richer and more ambiguous. Modern design must interact not only with nature but with the massive human revisions of nature: the city, technology, and other established designs that jostle for pride of place. Social designs as well as material designs: governments, corporations, religions, self-contained value-systems permeated by institutional self-interest. And more potent perhaps than any of these is a mass market that has little concern for nature or truth in its obsessive pursuit of profit.

Unnatural stresses can cause monumental design disasters. We have already met Hideyoshi, the ruler who was so nervous about the power of design that he killed a chief designer. In future pages we will encounter an architect who, disappointed in his clients, sought consolation in the riskiest of semiotic strategies and a software giant so paranoid about the possible loss of intellectual property that it deprived its own designers of indispensable knowledge. But we will also see that good design is still possible, that designers can still avail themselves of valid traditions, and that indeed the act of design is fundamental to the survival of our humanity.

To our task, then. How can design tell the truth to nature and avoid undue conflict with neighboring technologies? A product of good design

- is in accord with nature and human nature
- is in harmony with its immediate environment
- converses with contingent technologies
- helps to develop skill and/or imparts knowledge
- extends the user's sensibilities and freedom
- projects simplicity
- minimizes difficulties and dangers
- conveys a sense of beauty
- gives pleasure to use
- is not unreasonably expensive
- is sustainable
- allows its user to perform optimally in engaging reality
- can be delivered, installed, and repaired conveniently

Not all design products can be measured by all these guidelines. My comfortable Ekornes easy chair does not help me "develop skill" except by affording me the rest necessary for future skill development. Despite such exceptions, the guidelines seem broadly applicable. Later we will see that they even come in handy in philosophical disputation. Indeed, good design is pragmatic philosophy in action—except that it is an erotic pragmatism, an ethic of practice that honors the dominion of beauty and delight. This way, too, it tells us the truth about ourselves.

Designing Verbal Truth

If all design is truth-telling, we should find special relevance in our own designs of self-expression. Good artists are major truth-designers, working with brushes, chisels, and other essential media. For those of us who tell the truth in print, the primary designing instrument has become the word processor. Although various word processors have much in common, I have special reasons for preferring Word-Perfect X3. To understand why, we must remember John Heskett's . dictum that a well-designed tool becomes an extension of the senses. In other words, good design renders itself invisible while simultaneously magnifying the scope of its user's will. WordPerfect X3 does this. It enables me to express my thoughts, preserve them, and convey them to others without fighting me along the way. Unlike other word processors, whose defects often reflect the influence of top-down corporate priorities, X3 successfully reflects design choices focused on that oft-forgotten soul, the user. It tells me that my thought matters and that I can keep improving it. In doing so, it tells me the truth about writing.

By comparing WordPerfect X3 with its much-better-selling rival, Microsoft Word, we can experience an object lesson in the difficulties of designing for a complex and contentious marketplace. Although the two word processors look similar at first glance, a few weeks of professional use reveal four areas in which WordPerfect X3 is more powerful. It easily opens alien files. It easily reveals the full assortment of hidden codes that otherwise could ruin the format of a page. It extends its full graphics potential into the production of labels and business cards. And its "Append" feature allows the user to copy multiple passages into the same temporary memory bank. Word 2007 has none of these features, although it has had ample means and opportunity to develop them.

Why such discrepancies? We may conjecture that modest-sized Corel, which makes WordPerfect X3, saw design excellence as the only way to survive, given the near monopoly of Microsoft. Presumably, Corel chose professional writers as its niche consumers, whereas Microsoft prioritized users who were into Internet surfing, business, music, and games. That is, market pressures—or at least perceived market pressures—led the smaller company to outstanding design achievement and led the larger to relative mediocrity. The irony here is that free-market dynamics have not exalted the clearly better and cheaper Corel product. For this anomaly, we must thank the legendarily adversarial strategies of Corel's larger rival. Good design may well tell the truth, but truth itself is often drowned out by mass-market cannonry.

How Design "Speaks"

When I characterize design as part of a dialogue with nature, I am availing myself of an interpretive tradition that dates back to Renaissance humanism. Humanism was a knowledge-based program whose goal was to replace the feudal system with representative government and, more implicitly, to replace faith with reason. This mission ultimately produced the great democratic states of the West. Humanists saw language—spoken and written—as the life-principle of a healthy state. They built on this premise by adopting the Latin classics as models and developing an educational system of language arts that would establish knowledge, literacy, and eloquence as key political virtues. Ultimately they developed a universal culture in which all the arts and sciences interacted and evolved around common structures of discourse.

Small wonder that thought and action in the Renaissance were alive with metaphors of speech and dialogue. State governments were named after speech-acts (Parliament, Sala della Ragione). Civic leaders were known as *oratores*. Miscellaneous disciplines were presented in books known as "theaters": theater of chemicals, theater of maps, theater of comets, theater of nature, theater of machines, theater of the world. Emblem makers wove language into strange complexes of visual signs. Theorists revived Horace's statement "Ut pictura poesis" (As with painting, so with poetry). Engineers created statues that seemed to sing. Claudio Monteverdi made operatic history by subordinating musical meaning to the power of words.

By the High Renaissance it was realized that art and architecture could "speak"—convey specialized moral and psychological meanings—to receptive audiences. Leon Battista Alberti, working in the fifteenth century, made much of the connection between visual art and narrative. Giulio Romano created the Palazzo Te, a building that was at once masonry and an embodied flight of fancy, based in part on Ciceronian rhetoric and designed to function as a liberating influence on all who were lucky enough to be invited there. A visiting emperor, Charles V, was so dazzled that he promptly promoted Giulio's patron, the marquis of Mantua, to duke. Charles's grandson Emperor Rudolf II built in Prague an even grander monument to the complex language of visual meanings, including the world's first museum, where Giuseppe Arcimboldo created extravagant emblematic art and designed, in the manner of Giulio, multidimensional court masques. By 1612, the year of Rudolf's death, the idea of design as a symbolic language had spread as far as the British Isles, where the language of design was evident in the work of the architect and theatrical designer Inigo Jones. Although Renaissance artists and artisans did not put the principle in so many words, they believed that design could "tell the truth" about our humanity, our continuity, and our connection to nature.

This tradition persists today, although the message is often suppressed by the din of the modern marketplace. Christopher Alexander, in the influential book, *A Pattern Language: Towns, Buildings, Construction,* demonstrates that serious designers are still conveying spatial and visual messages to their clients.[1] More recently, Paul Graham has remarked that whole cities speak to us:

> Great cities attract ambitious people. You can sense it when you walk around one. In a hundred subtle ways, the city sends you a message: you could do more; you should try harder.
>
> The surprising thing is how different these messages can be. New York tells you, above all: you should make more money. There are other messages too, of course. You should be hipper. You should be better looking. But the clearest message is that you should be richer.
>
> What I like about Boston (or rather Cambridge) is that the message there is: you should be smarter. You really should get around to reading all those books you've been meaning to.[2]

My purpose in Part One is to expand the study of material language from the arts to design in general, to determine whether various designs that we create tell the truth or lie, and to show why and how they do so.

4

Design as Tragedy:
The Rise and Fall of the Twin Towers

In other words, Osama, the renegade son of the Bin Laden
building dynasty, not only attacked the symbol of capitalism but
also the symbol of the cultural inflation of Islamic architecture,
an inflation to which his own family has been party. It's a devilish
imbroglio beyond the stretch of any literature, fantasy or divine
conspiracy theory. Who says architecture has lost its significance?
One could almost wish it had less significance.

OLE BOUMAN

When Sen no Rikyu defied authority and sealed his unique message
with his own blood, he left his contemporaries with a design statement
that inspired posterity for centuries. More often, however, designers
strive to please their clients and alter their designs if the clients are
not satisfied with them. The municipal and corporate architecture
of our cities is less the result of auteuristic design conceptions—or
general design principles—than of various down-and-dirty vectors
in intersection: budgetary issues, profit projections, committee politics, competitive dynamics, and personality factors. In most cases,
key players muddle through to agreement, and the product of their

consensus is, if not inspiring, livable. In rare but edifying cases, however, designers attempt to compensate for their compromises with an excess of ingenuity and are confronted with what Edward Tenner calls "unintended consequences": "It is the tendency of the world around us to get even, to twist our cleverness against us. Or is it our own unconscious twisting against ourselves. Either way, wherever we turn we face the ironic unintended consequences of mechanical, chemical, biological, and medical ingenuity—revenge effects, they might be called."[1]

Consider, for example, the World Trade Center in New York. In this mammoth project, financial and political interests brought about a distortion of design that led to a colossal architectural blunder. The idea for the World Trade Center took root in 1946, when the New York State legislature set up the World Trade Corporation to accommodate the flood of commerce that would predictably spring from the rebuilding of postwar Europe. Although this initiative died in planning, the concept of a world trade center reemerged in 1958, with motives that were strategically more specific. David Rockefeller at Chase Manhattan Bank saw his company's downtown real-estate investments slipping and decided that a massive commercial project would bolster their value. He consulted with the architectural firm of Skidmore, Owings and Merrill, who drafted a plan. As one writer describes it, "Rockefeller sent the report on to Mayor Robert F. Wagner, and called Skidmore, Owings and Merrill right back. He was intrigued by the trade center idea and wanted to know more. By January of 1960, DLMA [Downtown–Lower Manhattan Association] had in hand a proposal for a $250 million trade center to be erected on a 13-acre site at the east end of Wall Street. It was to include a 70-story office-hotel building, an international trade mart for the exhibition of goods, a securities exchange building, a retail arcade, and a large plaza, all built upon a two-story platform that would supersede and displace the conventional street grid."[2]

By the time the project was set before the architect Minoru Yamasaki, it had been taken over by the Port Authority and had grown even more immense: "The program presented to Yamasaki, who was selected over a dozen other American architects, was quite explicit: twelve million square feet of floor area on a sixteen acre site, which also had to accommodate new facilities for the Hudson tubes and subway connections—all with a budget of under $500 million."[3] Yamasaki looked over a hundred potential plans in model form. In due course he approached his clients with the model of a complex crowned by two 80-story towers. But 80 stories were not enough for Lee Jaffe and Guy Tozzoli of the Port Authority: "It was Tozzoli who determined the program for the project, which called for an astonishing ten million square feet of office space. . . . It was Tozzoli, moreover, who adopted a suggestion from the Port Authority's public relations director, Lee K. Jaffe, to make the Trade Center's buildings the tallest in the world; he insisted that Yamasaki enlarge his proposal for 80-story towers to a pair of twin 110-story structures, with four million square feet of office space apiece."[4] The Port Authority's insistence on building the tallest buildings in the world forced Yamasaki to rethink his towers stylistically and structurally. The result was a plan that stretched the concept of the skyscraper as an economic engine at once space-saving and spectacular to an extent almost undreamed of. It would stack 220 acres of office space onto two acres of real estate.

The metropolitan implications of this change in plans were ominous. Yamasaki's original 80-story towers would have fitted gracefully into the high end of the Lower Manhattan skyline along with Forty

Wall Street and the American International Building, both about 70 stories tall. Towers 110 stories tall, on the other hand, would dwarf these buildings and tyrannize the rest of the skyline. The Twin Towers, in both height and breadth, would confound the scale of the neighborhood and explode the urbane Manhattan vernacular like a pair of hurled expletives. Yamasaki might well have complained that after such gross revisions, his towers were not "designed" at all but were (as they say of the camel) engineered by committee.

There were humanitarian implications as well. Creating workspace for tens of thousands of people on two acres means crowding, and crowding demeans and alienates. And the higher the building, the more dangerous it becomes in times of catastrophe; both escape and access become more limited. The latter consideration was apparently of little importance to the Port Authority managers. Eager to enlarge the rental space, they cut the emergency escape routes for each building from six down to three.

The Port Authority did this even though each of the most likely forms of emergency—fire, nuclear attack, and earthquake—would have put the elevator system at risk. The moneymaking gambit had dramatic effects on September 11, 2001. If the Port Authority had stuck to the six-stairway code, they probably would have put one stairway at each corner of each tower, instead of bunching the three stairways together in the center of each floor. No air attack would have been able to block all the passages of escape unless it destroyed the entire floor. As it turned out, the attack of 9/11 paralyzed the elevators, destroyed all three stairways in the North Tower above the ninety-fourth floor and two of the three stairways in the South Tower above the seventy-eighth floor (fewer than twenty people escaped down the third). Given the entry paths of the two planes that slammed into the towers, if six stairways had been built, including four at the tower corners, at least one stairway would have been left open in each tower, saving hundreds of lives.

The Port Authority's pocketbook determined another key design decision. Yamasaki's engineers presented its managers with a plan that employed a tube structure, placing key support elements on the skin of each building. As one of the engineers, Leslie Robertson, remembered, "The Port Authority liked it because it gave them large, unobstructed floor-plates." In exchange for extra rental room, however, interior support was reduced. Because the floor beams were made of thinner steel than the support columns, they heated up faster—a critical weakness when fire spread. This "flimsy" floor system collapsed in the 9/11 fires.[5]

An inevitable result of Yamasaki's tubular support structure was the comprehensive loss of window space. The external support system necessitated uncomfortably narrow windows, windows all but invisible in exterior photographs of the buildings, windows so inadequate that they offered barely any view from inside. Yamasaki, who had to take a good measure of criticism for this design strategy, protested feebly that his purpose had been to lessen the vertigo that might otherwise have afflicted denizens of the towers. But this excuse was directly contradicted by Robertson, his own engineer, who said that Yamasaki had gone for the tubular idea because it reminded him of bamboo and that the Port Authority had opted for it simply because it maximized rental space. The result of this strategy was a modern contradiction in terms, a pair of colossi that towered above the world's choicest view but were nonetheless legally blind. A political satirist could not have chosen a better symbol for the corporate conception of free enterprise.

One final element of the World Trade Center design deserves special attention because it links Yamasaki directly to the Saudi royal family and indirectly to Osama bin Laden. At the time that he received the World Trade Center commission Yamasaki had just finished building the Dhahran Air Terminal in Saudi Arabia, which had been contracted out to the Bin Laden construction company.[6] Its styling was a blend of Islamic architectural ideas and modern engineering. With the World Trade Center, Yamasaki achieved something similar.

Yamasaki described its [the World Trade Center's] plaza as "a mecca, a great relief from the narrow streets and sidewalks of the surrounding Wall Street area." True to his word, Yamasaki replicated the plan of Mecca's courtyard by creating a vast delineated square, isolated from the city's bustle by low colonnaded structures and capped by two enormous, perfectly square towers—minarets, really. Yamasaki's courtyard mimicked Mecca's assemblage of holy sites—the Qa'ba (a cube) containing the sacred stone, what some believe is the burial site of Hagar and Ishmael, and the holy spring—by including several sculptural features, including a fountain, and he anchored the composition in a radial circular pattern, similar to Mecca's.

The "shimmering filigree" of the trade center facade was the "mark of the holy," continues the architect Laurie Kerr, who quotes the Islamic scholar Oleg Grabar. According to Grabar, Kerr says,

The dense filigree of complex geometries alludes to a higher spiritual reality in Islam, and the shimmering quality of Islamic patterning relates to the veil that wraps the Qa'ba at Mecca. After the attack, Grabar spoke of how these towers related to the architecture of Islam, where "the entire surface is meaningful" and "every part is both construction and ornament." A number of designers from the Middle East agreed, describing the entire façade as a giant "mashrabiya," the tracery that fills the windows of mosques.

With these design elements, Yamasaki made a semiotic statement that he apparently intended to be a tribute to the Islamic tradition in particular and to the continuity of human design in general. He was tragically unaware that this statement could be interpreted in other ways as well. As Kerr concludes,

> To someone who wants to purify Islam from commercialism, Yamasaki's implicit Mosque to Commerce would be anathema. To Bin Laden, the World Trade Center was probably not only an international landmark but also a false idol.[7]

To an Islamic fundamentalist with a knowledge of architecture, Yamasaki's creation violated sacred information codes. Islamic law forbids the unauthorized "quotation" of the holy: the use of holy meaning in secular media. Muslims may carry charms containing verses of the Qur'an, but the verses must be sealed tight, never read. Penalties for misusing holy meanings can be severe. The Salman Rushdie case is only one example. Marcel Khalife, a popular singer, was arrested and tried in Lebanon for quoting a Qur'anic verse in one of his songs, even though the song was pro-Islamic. More recently, a teacher, Gillian Gibbons, was arrested in Sudan for allowing her class to name an imaginary bear Muhammad.

Yamasaki's public pronouncement about his massive project is worth noting. Although he had every reason to bemoan the effects of bureaucratic interest, vulgar hype, and pure greed on his original design, he put on a game face and touted his twin colossi as humanistic monuments: "The World Trade Center should, because of its importance, become a living representation of man's belief in humanity,

Lockheed Constellation. Courtesy of Lockheed Martin
Aeronautics Company.

1954 Buick Century. Courtesy of Lee Suttles.

Adolf Hitler, *Landscape*, 1919.

Winston Churchill, *View of Carcassonne.* Reproduced with
permission of Anthea Morton-Saner on behalf of
Churchill Heritage Ltd. Copyright © Churchill Heritage Ltd.

Giulio Romano, Sala dei Gigante (detail). Museo Civico
di Palazzo Te, Mantova. Photograph by author.

Pedro Berruguete, *Portrait of Duke Federico da Montefeltro.* Ducal Palace, Urbino.

Sofonisba Anguissola, *Self-Portrait with Bernardino Campi.* Pinacoteca Nazionale, Siena. Photograph by author.

his need for individual dignity, his belief in the cooperation of men, and through this cooperation his ability to find greatness."[8]

Few statements in the history of architectural interpretation are so provocative or so questionable. Invoking "humanity" and "individual dignity" strikes an especially hollow note. I have never heard or read of anyone else associating these terms with the Twin Towers.[9] Opinion, in fact, leans toward the contrary: that the towers were oppressive and intimidating, that they violated the preexisting skyline of Lower Manhattan, that they baldly and crudely asserted corporate power, and that (by implication) they demeaned humanity and ignored the individual. Early on, the towers were seen as bludgeons of institutional power. Here is Roger Cohen, writing in 1990: "The Trade Center project was widely denounced as a supreme example of self-glorifying monumentalism on the part of unaccountable, autonomous public authorities. Lingering resentment over its perceived excesses continues, two decades after its opening, to color public attitudes about the Port Authority."[10]

Not even the most poignant of eulogies after the towers' collapse in 2001 credits them with humanity or affirmation of individuality. If they were beloved at all, it was not for these qualities but because they symbolized in a gargantuan sense the bustle, vitality, and power of New York City. As the *Asia Times* put it, "The twin towers of the WTC were more than just buildings. They were a living testament of New York's faith in its own boundless destiny. Built more than 30 years ago through sheer power of will at a time when New York's future seemed uncertain, and in the face of weak demand, the towers restored confidence and helped bring a halt to the decline of Lower Manhattan. Brash, glitzy and bigger than life, they quickly became symbols of a tenacious New York, the city of superlatives in a nation of superlatives." "Brash, glitzy and bigger than life"? No question. But these qualities, as many critics of American culture have observed, do not add up to humanity and individual dignity. Ada Louise Huxtable shrewdly observed in 1973, "The Port Authority has built the ultimate Disneyland fairytale blockbuster. It is General Motors gothic." Huxtable's evaluation has since been corroborated by the likes of Martin Filler and Robert Hughes.[11]

This disparity between Yamasaki's intention and his actual achievement raises some interesting issues in modern design and modernity itself. The Port Authority mandate that crossed his desk subjected all other considerations—safety, the skyline, the environment, beauty, human space—to the enhancement of commerce. This blunt emphasis may strike readers as cold-blooded, but it is so characteristic of American corporate thinking that it is all but taken for granted by bureaucrats, planners, and designers. Yamasaki submitted a relatively humane proposal, but when it was rejected, he dutifully erected on a postage stamp of real estate a workplace that could hold the population of Venice, Italy. Perhaps eager to respond to early criticism or else awed by his own exercise of enormous power, he was somehow able to romanticize this temple of commercialism as a monument to humanity and the individual.

What Yamasaki actually achieved was quite different. In building the Twin Towers, he effectively ran into the ground a form of architectural rhetoric that had long saved the skyscraper from ignominy. The skyscraper, slim and soaring, had taken on a quasi-heroic role as mediator between us as individuals and the ever-increasing impingement of machines and crowds. It invited us to rise above the otherwise crushing power of mass interactions, in this way becoming part of a rhetoric of urban and corporate socialization. There is no question that Cass Gilbert's neo-Gothic Woolworth Building (1913), Raymond Hood's art deco RCA Building (1933), and the Ludwig Mies van der

Rohe–Philip Johnson high-modern Seagram Building (1958) are each artful enough to soften the impact of the corporate world on the individual. The problem lies only in the extent to which, as onlookers and participants, we can suspend our disbelief. Yamasaki overwhelmed our willing belief in the illusion. He exceeded the endurable ratio of mass to character. Without meaning to, he drew the rhetorical curtain away, laying bare, behind the blandishments of masonry, the operations of faceless power. Americans can accept power as a fact of life but refuse, from time to time, to defer to power automatically. This distaste for power helps explain the widespread criticism of the Twin Towers as an architectural statement.

Was the statement a truth or a lie? In one sense, the towers were not a lie at all: they were as inhuman as they looked. But they told an architectural lie in two ways.

Physically, they violated the humane commitments that were written into stone by Louis Sullivan and are assumed to be at the heart of all modern commercial architecture: the promises of safety, efficiency, and convenience. Examining the motives of the Port Authority from even the most charitable of perspectives, we find no evidence that they gave the slightest priority to these commitments. The result of their strategies had all the trappings of a medieval nightmare: unstable, inhibiting, ugly, unsafe.

Semiotically, their garbled design language and oppressive mass gave the lie to their architect's claim that the World Trade Center represented "man's belief in humanity" and "his need for individual dignity." To the contrary. Whether Yamasaki was lying to the public or merely to himself is a matter for his biographers. In either case, his statement, like the Twin Towers themselves, was typical of the lies that Big Money tells the public so that the public will not restrict Big Money from its earnest and unceasing quest for more of itself.

Still, none of us was going to knock them down. The impulse to destroy the towers, indeed, to turn their destruction into a symbolic holocaust of democracy, came from a tradition wholly different from that of American anti-authoritarianism. Born in Saudi Arabia around 1957, Osama bin Laden studied engineering in Jedda, a hotbed of Islamic radicalism, where he was exposed to such fundamentalist manifestos as Wail Uthman's *The Party of God in Struggle with the Party of Satan* and Sayyid Qutb's *Milestones*. Young Bin Laden imbibed a form of Islam that was shot through with notions of power and control: control of diet, dress, morality, sexuality; power exercised by fathers, clerics, prophets, and, above all, the supreme autocrat of history, the unquestionable Allah. The Arabic word *Islam* itself means "surrender": the individual's surrender to the All-Powerful. Worshippers are promised an eternal paradise in which they, via a reverse rhetoric of control, can enjoy the dominating and deflowering of lovely maidens.

Like Yamasaki, Bin Laden was professionally involved with architecture, but for Bin Laden, involvement carried a compulsive urgency. He is reported to have undergone a spiritual conversion as a teenager while helping his family restore two famous mosques. Yamasaki, who during Bin Laden's youth was working with Bin Laden's own family to westernize Saudi public architecture, could have seemed like some sort of Darth Vader to the boy—a figure who at once threatened his ideals and wielded massive authority.

Bin Laden, we may assume, grew obsessed with Yamasaki's Twin Towers, probably identifying them as both sources and symbols of Satanic power. On top of their assertion of capitalism, their phallic vanity, and their obtrusive nationalism, the towers were profanations of Islam. In this reading, his destruction of the towers becomes weirdly personal: a blow against the Party of Satan combined with a sideswipe at his own estranged family. Considering all of the Twin Towers' other structural and symbolic characteristics, it is hard to imagine two more likely targets for destructive extremism.

This montage of conflict and coincidence brings us back to our chapter title, "Design as Tragedy." Hegel wrote that tragedy arises from the clash of conflicting moral paradigms. The story of the World Trade Center, by this definition, is tragedy incarnate. It is a story played out by big personalities with starkly differing perspectives. There is the sagacious money manager, David Rockefeller, oiling the wheels of commerce. There are the bureaucrats, Guy Tozzoli and Lee Jaffe, shouldering their way ahead in the race for economic supremacy. Arrayed against them are the suicidal minions of Osama bin Laden, heir to a morally bankrupt fundamentalism. And trapped among them, the most tragic hero of them all, is the celebrated Minoru Yamasaki, who, caught in the wheels of power, lost perspective and compromised his own artistic integrity. We have numerous examples of designers (Sen no Rikyu among them) whose good intentions are betrayed by the base interests of their clients, but here we have something more darkly edifying: a designer who bought into his own betrayal.

There are tragic ironies as well: the irony that both the Twin Towers' creator and their destroyer had ties to the same family; the irony that an architectural homage to the Islamic design tradition should be interpreted as a profanation of it. But the greatest irony of all—an irony worthy of Conrad's *Heart of Darkness*—is that in an allegedly progressive and well-protected society, the major actions in this epic drama were performed with unconscionable crudeness: Osama bin Laden confused sanctity with slaughter, and the Port Authority managers believed that bigger was better and put thousands of lives at risk for the sake of more rental space. That ignorance and greed on this scale were allowed to determine our history does America no credit.

Edsel's Law:

How Bad Design Happens

Well-designed objects are easy to interpret and understand.
They contain visible clues to their operation. Poorly-designed objects
can be difficult and frustrating to use. They provide no clues—
or sometimes false clues. They trap the user and thwart
the normal process of interpretation and understanding.

DONALD NORMAN

A building or object should let you use it how you want:
a good building, for example, will serve as a backdrop for whatever
life people want to lead in it, instead of making them live
as if they were executing a program written by the architect.

PAUL GRAHAM

An excellent reason for staying in decent shape well into middle age is that you might have to prevent a man from getting crushed to death in your kitchen. To this cautionary adage, and how it relates to commercial design, I will return in a moment.

There are two main sources of good design and three main sources of bad design. Good design happens when corporations care about design and designers care about users. Bad design results from ignorance, poor socioeconomic resources, and skewed professional priorities. The first two do not require exposition. The last three do.

Ignorance

My experience with desktop computers suggests to me that computer designers rarely, if ever, listen to the people who do repair work on computers after warranty. If they did, they would realize that a major source of computer crashes in machines two or more years old is the accumulation of dust that has been sucked in by the cooling fans. Obviously, air filtration is the answer. Engineers may protest that filtration is a safety risk because clogged filters cause overheating. But this problem can be solved with one of technology's simplest devices: a heat switch that generates an alarm and/or shutdown if the cooling system begins to fail. In other words, many computer crashes are the result of manufacturers' ignorance of their products' performance over time.

Poor Resources

How many good commercial designs came out of Soviet Bloc countries between 1945 and 1990? I cannot find a single one in any of my design books. This suggests that when free thought and free enterprise are choked off, and economies struggle, design is among the first casualties.

Skewed Priorities

Of the three major causes of poor design, this one is the most complex and interesting. We have already seen how corporate priorities tempted tragedy at the World Trade Center. Now let us consider some subtler and more homespun ways in which the front office can ruin the design of a product. We should keep in mind that corporate designs observe the model of rock, paper, and scissors. Front-office priorities are rocklike, and design is often forced to wrap around them like paper, only to be cut by the scissors of real-world use—which in turn may be crushed by front-office priorities.

This conundrum was brought home to me with dangerous consequences in the spring of 2004, shortly after Lowe's hardware store delivered my new GE refrigerator. The crate was dollied up my drive by two delivery men big enough to play offensive line for the Philadelphia Eagles. These giants unsheathed the new appliance on the front deck—it looked slightly odd to me, but more of that later—then came inside to remove the old one.

But once inside the kitchen they began muttering and shaking their heads.

"Sorry, man," said the even bigger lad, pointing to my ancient seven-foot-tall Sub-Zero, "we can't touch this one."

I protested that I'd told Lowe's specifically what kind of unit had to be removed, but the delivery men assured me that internal communications were not part of their shop protocol.

After they left I called the moving companies. They would do it, but for a fee big enough to buy a second refrigerator.

Then I thought of Bill Colt, that intrepid jack of all trades. He lived three hours' drive away, owned a large van, and could recruit his labor at reasonable expense. Reached at his home, he remembered the Sub-Zero from an earlier visit and assured me that hauling it off would be no problem.

Around noon the next day Bill showed up with a hand truck and his crew, a smallish wiry man named Les. We three stood in the kitchen for a few minutes, contemplating the old beast and debating exit routes. Soon deciding that Bill would dope it out somehow, I escaped into the study and sat down to write.

Since the study is just across the front hall from the kitchen, I could glance up now and then to follow their progress. At one point I found the men and the machine in a particularly ungainly posture. Bill was near the kitchen's exterior door, tugging at the Sub-Zero's base, while poor Les was holding up the top and guiding the dolly at the same time.

At that moment Les collapsed and began squealing for help. He'd lost his footing, and the full weight of the refrigerator was crushing him to the floor. I jumped up and scrambled over to him. I had a lucky angle and was able to lift the thing a few inches, enough for him to squirm out from under.

The rest of the replacement operation went without incident. After Bill and Les had left, I had leisure to admire the new refrigerator that they had just installed. My previous qualms were immediately confirmed. It looked like God's wrath. It was one of those face plate models, and it had come without the face plates. Neither I, who had chosen it on the GE Web site, nor the Lowe's appliance man who had ordered it, had seen any warning indicating that further parts or assembly was necessary.

The face plates took months to ship and cost a bundle.

What did this harrowing event have to do with design? Everything. The construction of a refrigerator that could easily maim or kill its deliverers was, most likely, the result of a front-office priority. Sub-

Zero had its market niche among high-end, counter-depth "designer" refrigerators. A counter-depth refrigerator is shallow enough not to break the profile of the kitchen counters; hence it presents a "designed" appearance. For even greater snob appeal, these units can be ordered with face plates that mimic the wood surfaces—oak, cherry, maple—of existing cupboards. But the counter-depth refrigerator puts special constraints on its designers. Shallowness eats up space and necessitates a wider profile. Sub-Zero added not only width but height and met the resultant cooling demands by putting a second compressor on top of the refrigerator. The designers fulfilled their priorities, but in so doing they created a monster.

It was the weight of the second compressor that put Les in such a desperate position on my kitchen floor.

The moral of this story is that front-office priorities and good design do not always mix. Nor are front-office design disasters necessarily caused at the production end alone. When *user* front offices make arbitrary decisions about the design of products, they can temporarily usurp the power of the designer. The perils inherent in such decisions was demonstrated tragically in 1944 as the US Third Army planned its advance across Europe to Germany. The Allies could be confident of superiority over the German defenders in infantry, air support, supplies, and transport; but German armor, particularly the Tiger and Panther tanks, were a potentially dire threat. Lieutenant General George Patton, the Third Army commander, was faced with a momentous choice: equip his divisions with the Sherman M4 medium tank—which was relatively small and thinly armored—or with the newer Pershing M26 heavy tank, which was much more competitive with the Tiger and Panther in size, armor, and firepower. Over the objections of his experienced senior staff, Patton chose the Sherman; it was more reliable and maneuverable than the Pershing, he believed, and could be kept out of the range of German tanks. The Allies paid the price for this decision. In the combat that followed, German tanks zeroed in on the Shermans and destroyed hundreds in what was little more than target practice. The repeated US failures in armored confrontations, including this one, helped lead to the German counterattack, the Battle of the Bulge, with its 180,000 casualties.[1]

Even free designers, unencumbered by front offices and left to their own devices, can fall prey to their own priorities. Thomas Jefferson, for example, was an interesting architect but a quirky one. He was fascinated by octagons, and at Poplar Forest (near Lynchburg, Virginia) he built both a house and a privy in that shape. The architectural challenge presented by the octagon, and by other broad shapes like squares and circles, is what to do with the central space. Jefferson met this challenge with another unusual design idea: a central room shaped as a perfect cube, twenty feet wide, tall, and high. But what this room achieved in philosophical appeal (it was a Masonic symbol), it lost in livability.[2] The space is uninviting and vaguely institutional, with no natural light at eye level, and it must have been a bear to heat.

At Monticello, Jefferson indulged another of his idiosyncrasies, a dislike for central staircases, which he thought wasted space. But by conserving space he forced himself and his housemates to use dark, narrow stairs, inconveniently placed, that turned his three-story house into a firetrap. Moreover, the exclusion of a central stairwell, which could have fit easily into the large entrance hall, robs his house of the only feature that would have communicated between the public and the private spaces. One might suppose that Jefferson intended to protect his own privacy upstairs. Not so. His bedroom and his library were on the ground floor.[3]

A Proposal for an "Edsel Scale"

Dusty computers, top-heavy refrigerators, and quirky interiors—they all suggest that when a producer loses sight of rational use or insists on a narrow priority, bad things happen to design. Call this Edsel's law. If we rank firms or individuals that honor the principles of good design on an Edsel scale from -1 to -10, where -10 is the best score, and firms that neglect or even flout these principles from +1 to +10, where +10 is the worst score, Thomas Jefferson's two noblest political designs, the Declaration of Independence and the Statute of Virginia for Religious Freedom, would probably merit -10s, and his two homes would fare somewhat less gloriously. The Herman Miller Corporation, with its corporate commitment to good design (Aeron chair, Eames chair), would probably draw deep minus ratings. Sub-Zero, the maker of my demon fridge, would be high in the plus column for posing a threat to human life. But even Sub-Zero, mistaken as it was, did not deliberately insult design principles. That distinction belongs to a software company that I cannot name without compromising the privacy of my informant. So I will use false names.

Marta Hayward works for the software maker Regulus, a leader in its own market niche. In my e-mail from her, she describes the kind of organizational forces that affect her design policies: "Here, decision-making is so decentralized that if the legal equation of corporation and individual were pursued, companies might escape culpability by claiming insanity manifest in dissociated personality." Since nothing is as hazardous to good design as conflicting priorities, we can guess that Regulus is headed for some impressive Edsel numbers. According to Marta, a team at Regulus struggled to write a knowledge program called Genie! for a rival company, Slinkytracks, which wanted to run that software on its equally new operating system. The folks at Slinkytracks naturally wanted the best product possible, but they were so secretive about their new operating system that they gave Regulus almost no information to work with.

This was another case of conflicting priorities affecting the ultimate quality of a product. The villain here is Slinkytracks, not Regulus, but it is Regulus that will create the inferior software.

In Marta's early days at Regulus, "high level managers *concealed the intended users of the system from the development team* because they didn't want competitors to know through leaks what markets we were going after. They just came up with specs that we were supposed to develop to. It was a real struggle. The sales force did not want us to have contact with actual users for a host of reasons" (my emphasis). Here management is violating a fundamental design principle: optimal use. Designers are being prevented, by their own colleagues, from creating a product suitable to users' needs. Earlier I referred to the legendary designer Jef Raskin, who wrote that designers should behave as responsibly toward their clients as surgeons should behave toward their patients. At Regulus we have the equivalent of a surgeon told to operate without being told what is wrong with the patient. Load on a bunch of Edsel points.[4]

Although secrecy and even deception are occasionally permissible in competitive enterprise, it is downright weird when firms use these combative measures in ways that diminish the quality of their own products. The Boston Consulting Group brands such practices "compromises" in which an "industry imposes its own operating constraints on customers"; that is, the industry translates corporate confusion into public use.[5] Gaffes of this sort are particularly ironic in the knowledge business, where enlightenment and transparency are the topics of all advertising and the proclaimed goals of all enterprise.

Not only the advertising but the product itself becomes a kind of lie: a self-defeating technology, a poisoned medicine.

Though not expecting miracles, I suggest that issues such as those raised by Marta Hayward might be resolved, and design in the knowledge business greatly improved, by a few simple organizational reforms. Corporate leadership should be more attentive to the policies and practices of design teams. Corporate marketing teams should maintain a high level of in-house accountability, transparency, and disclosure. Corporate activity on all levels should be value-driven, the ultimate goal or value being a product that benefits the user.

Happily, the crazy goings-on at Regulus do not apply to the whole knowledge business. Phenomena like Linux and Google proclaim that good design, compatibility, openness, and even generosity make up the most effective recipe for success in a forum that is based on information, learning, and discovery. Google's policies in this regard are especially noteworthy. Of all this company's many innovations, I can think of only one that does not conveniently enlarge its users' knowledge base.[6] Considering its many services, I cannot think of another knowledge source that so naturally speaks to the multifarious needs of the mind. The most important of Google's applications—including Web page design and hosting—are free of charge. This fact, along with Google's rapid and enormous financial success, suggests that the shortest way to winning in business lies in designing for optimal use and investing generously in increasing users' wealth of knowledge.

Google got its priorities straight and kept its eye on the ball. In so doing, it has become a landmark in the history of design.

6

Designs of Darkness

Wherefore by their fruits ye shall know them.

MATTHEW 7:20

I have contrasted Sen no Rikyu, a philosophical designer who held firm to his artistic values, with Minoru Yamasaki, an architect who disastrously complied with the dictates of the local power structure. But Yamasaki, whose rationalizations ranged from gross exaggeration to outright lie, was still a well-meaning sort who never made the injury of users a career goal. Now we will take a brief look at this darker phenomenon: the infiltration of abusive power into the mind of a designer. For this we will revisit that most authoritarian and dismissive of societies, Germany in the era of the Nazis.

When I say "dismissive" I mean brutally and programmatically so. The Nazis and similar rightist fanatics annihilated socialists like Rosa Luxemburg, liberals like Walther Rathenau, and moderates like Kurt von Schleicher. Persecution of Jews and Gypsies escalated, culminating in the death camps in 1941. Hitler could not even endure a rival presence among the other Fascists. His sympathizers assassinated the Nazi leader Ernst Röhm and the Austrian Fascist Engelbert Dollfuss in 1934. Röhm and Dollfuss were not eliminated for their politics. Their crime was not being Adolf Hitler.

Weaponry excepted, design in Germany fared no better than people. The famed Bauhaus school was officially denounced as degenerate, and its leaders, Walter Gropius, Ludwig Mies van der Rohe, and Paul Klee, all left Germany. Hitler had no use for progressive, cosmopolitan design and art. He wanted to bring German taste back to what he considered its correct stylistic bases: Roman imperialism and the Teutonic past. We have already seen him tinkering with Roman design in his massive Hall of the People project. Even more revealing, perhaps, will be a look into his mind as an artist. For Hitler was an accomplished draftsman who, early in life, tried to support himself by selling his art.

Hitler favored architectural studies, and his watercolor landscape presented here is no exception (see plate). It is the depiction of a small hill town. The choice of subject, complete with medieval towers and wall, suggests the atavistic nostalgia that characterized his thinking. The overall composition smacks of the postcard and other mass-market decorations. Hitler is so scrupulously careful with line that we feel we are viewing an art-school assignment. He is so intent on not blundering that he ignores the dazzling variety and complexities of light that many artists of his time were exuberantly exploring. Note also the emphasis on verticality. As though the facades, wall, and towers were not enough to convey the theme of height and power, Hitler establishes our vantage point with two columnar cypress trees.

Before we entertain any conjectures about the psychology of Hitler's art, let us sample the art of Hitler's great antagonist in England, Winston Churchill (see plate). Churchill took up painting in his forties and pursued it for almost fifty years. He enjoyed painting immensely and, unlike Hitler, was regarded as a museum-quality artist. His paintings sold and were hung prominently even when he submitted them under an alias. The view of Carcassonne before our eyes (which resembles Hitler's *Landscape* in many elementary details) is exemplary of his attitude and technique. Churchill, who claimed that art should be audacious, follows the impressionist mode, rejecting accuracy and correctness for a lively interplay of light and color. Yet the sense of form is so compelling that it binds the play of color into an interesting dialectic. In contrast to Hitler's severe linearity are Churchill's off-line and rounded-off renderings of the town buildings; the effect, together with the warm tones, gives the town the look of a living thing. In contrast to Hitler's cypress trees, which are distinguished only by their verticality, Churchill's cypresses are licked by sinuous flames of sunlight.

Granted, Hitler was using watercolors and Churchill used oils. But even so, a comparison between the two works is psychologically charged. Hitler's landscape is a testament to control: the control of architecture over nature, of walls over human beings, of vertical over horizontal, and (perhaps) the control of the teachers who had taught him not to deviate from linear accuracy. Churchill's landscape is a nuanced expression of joy, the statement of someone who, at ease with society and at home with art, can indulge himself in a testament to nature. While Hitler's design imprisons energy, Churchill's design releases it. Could it be pure coincidence that the most prominent defender of liberty in the twentieth century had these characteristics as an artist?

As with artistic form, so with artistic temperament. For Churchill, painting was a delightful escape from work. But Hitler's art could not escape the prison that was Hitler's mind.

A similar macro-micro resemblance is apparent in the German philosophy of the 1920s and 1930s. The four most influential works by German-speaking philosophers of the period were Ludwig Wittgenstein's *Tractatus* (1921), Martin Buber's *I and Thou* (1923), Martin Heidegger's *Being and Time* (1927), and Karl Popper's *The Logic of Scientific Discovery* (1934). Wittgenstein, Buber, and Popper, all of whom had Jewish backgrounds, accepted university positions outside Germany and Austria. Heidegger, however, stayed in Germany and eagerly took up the Nazi cause. Achieving influence at his home university in Freiburg, he joined others in persecuting Jews (including his own professorial mentor, Edmund Husserl) and preached Hitler's gospel on a number of fronts. But after Germany's defeat in World War II, he seized on every opportunity to minimize his past involvement with Nazism.

This obfuscation was, to some extent, successful. For years the accepted line on him was that he was a great philosopher but politically confused.[1] But this line is now disintegrating, in part because it is, and always has been, based on two errors. The first is the assumption that philosophical inquiry is ever wholly free of politics. It cannot be, for the simple reason that philosophy cannot wholly alienate itself from social interactions. The second is the assumption, based apparently on careless readings, that Heidegger did not announce a political platform in his magnum opus, *Being and Time.* It turns out that Heidegger's book was not only politically charged but also very convenient to his times. In 1999, Johannes Fritsche took the trouble to study *Being and Time* in the light of comparative politics.

According to Fritsche, Heidegger's concept of the relationship between peoples and destiny is the same as Hitler's, as is Heidegger's view that peoples must embody fate and sweep all opposition aside. This is the political expression of Heidegger's famous coinage, *Dasein* ("there-being," that is, existential virtue).

In contrast to ordinary *Dasein* and inauthentic *Dasein,* authentic *Dasein* . . . realizes that there is a dangerous situation, and relates itself to the "heritage." In so doing, it produces the separation between the *Daseine* that have fate and those that do not, i.e., the inauthentic *Daseine.* In the next step authentic *Dasein* realizes that its heritage and destiny is the *Volksgemeinschaft,* which calls it into struggle. . . . After this, authentic *Dasein* hands itself down to the *Volksgemeinschaft* and recognizes what is at stake in the struggle. . . . Finally, authentic *Dasein* reaffirms its subjugation to the past and to the *Volksgemeinschaft* and begins the struggle, that is, the cancellation of the world of inauthentic *Dasein.*[2]

In context, "authentic *Dasein*" translates as Nazism, and "inauthentic *Dasein*" means the Nazis' current or future victims. (A *Volksgemeinschaft* was Hitler's ideal community.)

Fritsche bases this interpretation primarily on a reading of section 74 of *Being and Time.* Here we find Heidegger at his murkiest and most authoritarian, breeding concepts so unfriendly to common understanding that they must be translated neologistically: "thrownness," "existentiell," "factically," "equiprimordially."[3] What emerges after repeated readings is the image of a (presumably German) national spirit (*Dasein*) that can authenticate itself by reaching back into its own past, choosing a hero, and risking mortal danger. Thus, without specifically mentioning Hitler or the Nazi Party, Heidegger is supplying a generalized argument for their hegemony. Fritsche draws connections between these concepts and those of other right-wing theorists of the time, notably Carl Schmitt and Hitler himself.

More recently, Emmanuel Faye has added abundant documentation to the case against Heidegger in his *Heidegger: The Introduction of Nazism into Philosophy in Light of the Unpublished Seminars of 1933–1935.*

After unfolding a wealth of information about Heidegger's vigorous and extreme Nazism, Faye concludes: "In the work of Martin Heidegger, the very principles of philosophy are abolished. No place is left for morality, which is openly and radically annihilated. Respect for individual human life, the refusal of destruction, the inner scruple of conscience that, turning inward upon itself and measuring the responsibility for one's thoughts, words, and deeds, not to mention generosity and the giving of oneself—all those qualities essential to man, and that it is philosophy's vocation to cultivate and reinforce, are eradicated to make room for the exaltation of the 'hard race.'"[4]

We need not subject Heidegger's political extension of *Dasein* to academic analysis. As a template for social renewal, it deserves the same sort of scrutiny we should apply to designs of every type.[5] By all relevant standards, Heidegger's social program fails conspicuously. It is unsustainable, hugely expensive in terms of human capital, and full of pain and ugliness. By basing itself on the arbitrary term *destiny,* it fails to engage reality. It lends itself to inbreeding and degeneration, rather than to an optimization of genetic resources. It is an offense against nature and human nature. And, as the history of the Third Reich shows, it creates unprecedented dangers. Heidegger was not just a politically naive academician. He was a pretentious, bombastic, and bigoted theorist who bypassed self-awareness in a quest for power and control.

As it was for Hitler the artist, so also was it for Heidegger the thinker. Both shared with the meanest criminal the compulsion to enforce their will on their fellows. Left unhindered, power and the quest of power can permeate art and design down to their psychological roots. Hitler and Heidegger stand with the Japanese warlord Hideyoshi, whose appetite for power extended to the way he served his tea. Only the Rikyus of the world, the brave souls who are ready to face down authority, to show human decency, and to risk all, can maintain the integrity of design.

Let us acknowledge the full extent of Rikyu's achievement. In reinterpreting the tea ceremony, Rikyu turned a ritual festivity into a revolutionary medium of communication. In so doing, he changed the nature of communication itself, from a class-determined exchange of formalities to a knowledge-based dialogue of equals. This quiet innovation brought Japan into the modern world, opening a path for exchange and progress in a manner as historically pertinent as the invention of printing. Perhaps Hideyoshi was aware of these implications, seeing in Rikyu a threat to dictatorial rule and recognizing, to his own dismay, the design of liberty.

7

Face to Face with Design

"Man is born free," wrote Jean-Jacques Rousseau in 1762, "and everywhere he is in chains." Rousseau could not have known of Sen no Rikyu's progress in the quest for freedom two centuries earlier and possibly would not have agreed with Rikyu's modest and decorous initiative. Nonetheless, the two thinkers can be seen as part of the same progressive project. Both worked along the axes of design, truth, and power. In the tea ceremony, Rikyu designed a social interaction that would empower his culture. Rousseau, along with contemporaries like Benjamin Franklin and Thomas Jefferson, produced a series of tracts, declarations, and enactments that set out the design for the political institutions of liberty. By so doing, they illustrated the principle, central to this book, that design "shapes, regulates, and channels energy, empowering forces that might otherwise be spent chaotically." In the early twenty-first century, the premises of liberty and equality underpin most social thought, and the variously interpreted concept called "liberation" is championed (sincerely or otherwise) throughout the world. Throughout my life the dialogue between liberty and authority that design partakes of has been very much in play.

A Boyhood in Design

I had a dog who, for a brief shining moment in 1973, became a member of the design community. A Samoyed pup named Max, bred in the farmland near the main stem of the Willamette River, southeast of Eugene, Oregon. A frolicsome puff of white fur who at that time was all of four months old. Weekday mornings my wife and I would trek off to work, locking Max in the backyard, which we had just fenced with cedar. Because we knew that he'd get bored, we left him a few old toys to play with—colorful little items including a rubber duck and three painted building blocks. One sunny afternoon we returned home to an amazing sight. Max had scraped out a yard-long opening under the cedar fence, pushed his toys out through the opening until the toys were visible from the sidewalk, and arranged them, equidistant from each other, like items in a shop window. The scene was topped off by Max's snout, thrust out as far as possible through the opening into the midst of his own toy arrangement, its black tip glistening with excitement.

Who knows why he did this? Probably it was an effort to attract playmates. I've read of animals who, through study or training, achieved much more impressive tricks. There was, for example, the baboon of Assisi who, having studied the illustrious Buonamico Buffalmacco painting a fresco on a chapel wall, sneaked into the church one night, "leapt onto the scaffolding where Buonamico used to stand to work, and there took up the phials and emptied them one by one, made the mixtures, broke as many eggs as were there, and began to daub all the figures with the brush, never resting until he had repainted everything himself."[1] But Max had never observed or studied advertising and display. His outburst of creativity derived from pure inspiration.

Max's genius came and went with puppydom. In later years he

was content to be a sedate fatherly companion or soft comfy pillow for little boys.

We have seen that design, employed wisely, can enable human liberty and, conversely, in the hands of a corrupt or abusive power, can suppress liberty. But we have not yet explored a third, less spectacular, but nonetheless essential link between design and power: the rush of empowerment felt by designers themselves in the execution of their visions. This experience is intimately connected with childhood; as children, we feel less uncomfortable about reinventing our private worlds. The thrill of creating or reshaping, though unlike any other sensation in human experience, is one that every child can enjoy and one that can bring delight and renewal to every person of whatever age. Such rushes of excitement may come in our early youth, when the world is still alive with great and mysterious presences. They may come later, when circumstance forces us to reconsider our personal technologies. Or they can come at any time when, struck with awe or amusement by some special artifact or contrivance, we are confronted with the native character of design. At such moments, we are faced with a long-hidden truth about ourselves: we have been endowed by nature with the ability to reshape our environment. At such moments, we are reintegrated in the human continuum and reminded of our hidden potentialities.

I became fascinated by the idea of design over several decades, moved by family necessity, professional experience, personal pleasure, and the slow seduction of chance events. My encounters with design have always been thrilling, marked by a feeling of being in special and intimate contact with the world around me.

At least, as I look back, it seems that way. My boyhood associates in Little Silver, New Jersey, included some quietly inventive types. On summer afternoons I'd sometimes join my neighbor Jimmy Harvey in paying a visit around the corner to his best friend, David Jansky. We would usually find David lounging in his backyard, sipping Coca-Cola from a tablespoon while he listened to Red Barber call a Brooklyn Dodgers game on the portable radio. It was in this backyard that Jimmy and David hatched the scheme that brought them neighborhood celebrity; putting on periodic fairs at Jimmy's house, complete with games of chance, treats, and prizes. Their precocious commercialism, staged with all the panache of hardened hucksters (Jimmy and David kept shouting, "And he wins a prize!"), entranced the younger kids and brought in piles of small change.

Then there was Johnny Parsons, the star of our class, who was good at everything, with the occasional exception of being good. As we reached puberty and began to think about the really serious aspects of life—women, tobacco, and alcohol—Johnny had the inspiration of turning the upstairs of his family's big garage into a fully equipped den of iniquity. Accordingly, together with three other classmates, we declared ourselves a club and began stocking the old apartment with every objectionable item we could lay hands on. Soon the mantelpiece sported a fifth of Four Roses; the floor was littered with *Esquires* and *Playboys*; and the air reeked of Prince Albert tobacco from my stylish slim-line Kaywoodie pipe. Our activities, which also included unauthorized driving practice in the Parsons family Jeep, went completely unnoticed by his family, the more surprisingly if you consider that Johnny's father was state attorney general.

At the time I did not consider David's or Jimmy's or Johnny's actions out of the ordinary. The fairs mounted by David and Jimmy were to me just another sign of their established street smarts. Johnny's depraved club struck me as simple good sense. And anybody who has ever tried it knows that cold Coke always tastes better when it is sipped from a tablespoon. I accepted these eccentricities as part of my familiar world.

And added my eccentricities as well. At age ten I penned a detailed treatise, now happily lost, about how to keep one's toes cool in bed. I created a book of graphics commemorating every grammar-school year. I found a way of converting a honeysuckle-covered treetop into a comfortable retreat. And, with fellow club member Barry Sherwood, I even invented a contact sport. It went like this: We each found an old thick-tire bicycle and removed the fenders. Every week we hoarded old newspapers. We waited for Sunday, when the village food market's parking lot was empty. Then, arriving at said parking lot on our bikes, we rolled the newspapers into fourteen-inch bats. Each with a bat in his right hand, we got on our bikes and engaged in a latter-day version of knightly combat, bashing each other with all our might about the head and shoulders. The rider who went down first lost the round.

Barry and I beat up on each other in perfect friendship. Barry was the kid whose normal greeting to me was, "Hi, Robby! Wanna wrassle?"

Above and beyond our humble contraptions were the commercial designs that affected our youth. My classmates and I did not know it, but we were riding a historical wave. The schoolchildren of the 1940s were the first generation born into the age of skyscrapers and the first generation born into an era when industrial design was an established specialty. After World War II the economy poured its billions back into commerce, and by the early 1950s the air was thick with novelties.

Many of these novelties entered my inner life. Without knowing it, I became part of a youth culture of design—a culture in which cleverly mass-crafted items held near-mystical significance. For me in 1954, a sixteen-year-old raised under prosperous circumstances but immured in a tiny suburb, commercial design offered moments of life-altering discovery and glimpses of a brilliant sphere beyond. In 1954 the introduction of the Parker Jotter forever transformed my favorite pastime, writing, although I stuck to the humble ink-filled Esterbrook fountain pen for nightly journal keeping. I cherished the rounded contours and ergonomic keyboard of the Royal Portable typewriter on the desk in my bedroom. These implements became the conduits for a binge of juvenile creative writing. The clean British lines and responsive handbrakes of my Rudge bicycle sang of space and freedom. Evenings I sat in my room doing homework or writing poetry to the tune of FM music from my new Philips radio, its stately facade lined with sexy ivory-colored pushbuttons. My Davis racket, with its slender throat and elegant aqua finish, improved my tennis style considerably. I took my first flight in the futuristically designed Lockheed Constellation (see plate). Even the six-ounce Coke bottle, with its precious content and its delightful palpability, spoke of a better world. And by the time I got to college, I had stocked up on khaki trousers, made famous by Gene Kelly in *An American in Paris* and then de rigueur on Ivy League campuses. Years down the line, Andy Warhol became the Homer of these design heroics. As a boy in the pre-Warhol era, I could only marvel at them.

The crowning event of my immersion in commercial design came that spring. My father, who had ordered a new Buick Century four-door hardtop, brought home the Buick catalog for family viewing (see plate). The 1954 model line was brand-new for GM, where head designer Harley Earl had ordered a communal flattening of hoods and trunk lids, a sweeping back of windshields, an annihilation of door frames, and an emphasis on performance. This innovative attitude would produce design classics like the first Corvettes and the '57 Chevies. But the '54 Buick Century, with its pleasantly sharky grille, its crisp but flowing contours, and its light frame resting on a two hundred horsepower V-8 engine, was classic enough for me. It was a four-wheeled rite of passage, a spiritual entry into the jet age. A year later it became the first family car I ever drove. On my maiden solo I made a point of driving it barefoot, maximizing the communion between machine and boy. For better or worse, I was bonding with my times.

A year later, my father added a white-on-black Buick Roadmaster convertible to the family fleet, and my senior year in high school became the Year of the Ragtop: my last year at home, my last year of boyhood, the last year I could experience the temperate chemistry of a small-town background. But when I passed from this measured climate into the hectic world of college and graduate school, I was unable to live with the esthetic and academic authorities that dominated these institutions of higher learning, and one of several neurotic symptoms was a complete shutdown of my own creative writing. I pulled my toys back in under the fence and did not push them out again for years.

Not wholly coincidentally, parallel lines of force were appearing in the macrocosm. By 1960 the commercial world, which had been so full of innovation in the middle 1950s, was opting for models of bourgeois security. The trim, economical lines of the '57 Chevy Bel Air were compromised in 1958, and then the model itself was replaced in 1959 by a monster chromed catastrophe that looked fit for the Dragon Lady.[2] Ford, which had dropped its brick with the Edsel (1958–60), failed to learn from this grim lesson and produced nothing but whales and hippos until the Mustang appeared in 1964. In general, American cars of the 1960s and 1970s were born in a closely monitored vacuum of ideas—a situation that discouraged some serious designers and forced others, like the young Jerry Hirshberg, to throw in their lot with foreign producers.[3]

Connected with these trends in design was a growing cultural malaise. The civil rights movement, the anti-Vietnam protests, and the hippies were all billed as responses to an American power structure that had grown blocklike, disingenuous, and manipulative. The antihero, played by James Dean, Paul Newman, or Steve McQueen, became the model in cinema, and various forms of real or pretended rebellion—pre-worn Levi's, skateboards, communes, and the drug culture—arose as alternatives to conventional lifestyles.

At the other end, corporate practices were growing increasingly dishonest and self-indulgent. In the 1960s the United States was not a major importer of oil; its balance of accounts with its trading partners was in the black, and it was the world's leading technological and manufacturing power. But all of these virtues—although we could not see it then, our attention being focused on other matters—had begun to slip. A generation later, we were the world's largest debtor nation; our addiction to imported oil and cheap gasoline increasingly determined our military commitments; the business of making things (the manufacturing sector) accounted for less than 20 percent of our economy, while the business of making money off of money (the financial sector) accounted for more than 30 percent; executive pay had reached obscene multiples of the average worker's salary; the tobacco companies' cynical strategy of inventing false doubt—over whether cigarettes cause cancer—had spread to such subjects as global warming, the theory of evolution, and the justification for invading foreign countries; deregulation and tax cuts had changed from tools for policymakers to ends in themselves; and many people staked their future not on prudently invested savings but on stock-market and real-estate bubbles. The collapse of the housing bubble brought on, in 2008, the worst financial crisis since the Great Depression, costing trillions in losses. Partly thanks to a federal administration that faithfully supported corporate policies, much of this greed and dishonesty persists.

Does this mean that the 1950s were better times than now? Such absolute comparisons are almost useless. It might be fair to say, however, that the 1950s, which saw the economic recovery from the Great Depression and World War II, produced a flurry of commercial innovations whose products were particularly apt to dazzle impressionable boys. From this point of view, we children of the 1950s were lucky. We and our commercial culture were young together.

The Bakers' Table

I have a theory about social class that goes like this: No matter how much money you make, you are upper class if you spend less than you earn, and you are lower class if you spend more than you earn. And if you spend exactly what you earn, give or take a hundred bucks or so a month, then you are anxious class.

My wife and I belonged to the anxious class while we were bringing up our kids. We worked hard and spent our monthly checks. The mortgage got paid, and bread was on the table. A pre-owned car was always parked on the steep driveway of our hillside house, presumably ready to head for campus or take kids to soccer. But ideas like buying a new car or taking a hotel vacation were out of the question.

Buying decent furniture was also well beyond our means. But lumber was cheap, so I started building tables. I designed an oak baby-changing table that was never used as such but came in handy for filling space. I designed a coffee table and an end table and had them assembled by the experts at a local wood shop called the Eugene Planing Mill.

Have I since become a famous furniture designer with merchandise for sale at Skymall.com? Not quite. But those tables taught me something. I realized that by designing them I had turned impoverishment into enterprise. I had transcended my own inhibiting academic world and briefly explored the material presences of daily life. I had freed my eyes and hands to converse with varieties of shape and substance. I had engaged my little world and changed it. For these reasons, there is something special for me about the practice of design.

My tables brightened up the living room and had a generally civilizing influence on the house. But we still had no dining table, and at a dining table I drew the line. My design talents did not extend to the gracious and the festive.

That's where Bill and Duffy Baker came in. They lived very near us in a big red house which, with its equally imposing red barn, sprawled over two acres at ridgetop. They owned a few retail businesses in the campus village, including Duffy's, the saloon of choice for fraternities and varsity athletes. Bill had a thing about furniture. His house was crowded with antiques and handmade pieces, including a classy four-poster bed. His barn was full of old stuff in various stages of restoration or decay.

A gala garage sale at the Baker barn in the late 1970s coincided, as it happened, with my peaking anxious-class frustration and semiannual lust to start making mischief with a piece of wood. When I told Bill that I needed a good dining table but could not pay much, he said, "Bob, I've got just the thing for you!" and led me back into the darkly stacked reaches of the Baker Barn, on the way trying to sell me his spare four-poster bed. A ray of sunlight in back caught the object of Bill's search, and soon I stood looking at the massive oak table that would become, more than I thought possible for an inanimate object, our family icon for the next quarter-century.

The table was a daunting prospect. Most of the original finish was missing, exposing wood that was alternately dried out or stained; patches of foggy shellac still clung to other areas. The five spiral-turned heavy legs (one to hold up extra leaves in the middle) looked solid enough but would require hours of cleaning up and staining. There were no extra leaves, and one of the dowels, which was supposed to slide into holes as the table was closed, was broken off. But worst of all was the veneer tabletop. Thumbnail-sized bits were missing altogether. Large areas of veneer, frayed at the edges and completely desiccated, had parted from the surface and curled inches into the air, as though in defiance of anyone brash enough to attempt a repair.

I said to Bill that it looked like a tough fix.

"Piece of cake, Bob. I'll talk you through it," he said, taking my hundred dollars.

For the next two months the table stood in my garage, getting attention. After much advice from Baker, my friend Bill Rockett, and others, I turned to the job of compelling the rampant veneer to sit down where it belonged. I moisturized the ancient sheet of wood until it was pliant but not soaked. Then I wiped off the liquid residue and pressed the veneer down in place on a bed of glue. I stabilized it with plywood, braced the job with a large cinder block, and left it overnight. This worked. When I removed the block and plywood the next morning, the thing in the garage looked like a table again.

That afternoon I picked up a small package of oak veneer and an Exacto knife at the Planing Mill, lined up grain with grain, and cut tiny pieces in the shape of each damaged portion of the surface. Once in place, these were also glued and braced.

Over the next few weekends, cutting a dowel, bleaching stains, removing old varnish, sanding, applying red oak finish, sanding again, finishing, sanding, finishing, I completed the restoration. No boredom in *that* job. Often at work I was suffused with quiet joy. The table was becoming a thing of beauty. I was bringing it back to itself.

Not that it wasn't also bringing things back to me. Restoring beautiful and useful things of the past—particularly items of family use—is about as close as we can get to restoring the past itself. The feedback is little short of spiritual. As I lavished care on the table I was taken back into the world of my earliest memories, when, in my grandparents' dining room on Hewes Street in Brooklyn, my head had gained enough altitude for me to notice that the big cherry-wood dining table was covered with a layer of glass. Occasionally this glass was lifted to allow for the insertion of some new piece of national history, clipped from a morning paper, the last of which was the shocking notice, complete with photograph, that President Roosevelt had died suddenly in Warm Springs, Georgia, on April 12, 1945.

It was at this glass-covered table, my legs dangling from the seat of a claw-foot chair, that I first took note of design and invention, when my grandfather Julius Carlson announced to me, in his high-pitched monotone, that he had invented the adjustable cap. He explained to me that he was a hat designer, told me what a hat designer did, and said that he worked for a hat factory and that there was some question about whether the factory owned rights to the invention or whether he did. Over the years that followed, Julius lost out in the legal wrangling, but until his death at ninety-one he had not the slightest doubt that he had been in the right, and for some years after hearing his story I could not look at an adjustable cap without a mixture of pride and regret.[4]

What finally became of my grandfather's glass-topped cherry-wood table? As I stroked on a second coat of shellac, I supposed that I could track it down, but to what good? Restoring my own table had brought me to see it with the eyes of the past, as only a child can see it, and now that image would be mine forever.

A few days later, when the finish had cured out, we carried Bill Baker's table out of the garage and set it down in the dining area, which looked east toward the kitchen counter and west toward a stand of Douglas firs. It was splendid. It completed the house as a family domain. And it stood in that spot for the next twenty-five years offering food and cheer as three boys grew up and three cycles of dogs, stretched out on a nearby carpet, listened to our friendly chatter as soothing music or were troubled by sudden stridencies. In my journal I describe a scene from the mid-1980s, when Ted, our youngest, was four years old and sitting at the oak table:

> 4/23/87— . . . Troubles with A & N vanished in the magic of the 15th & Onyx parting, but T opened a new canto by refusing to go to his daycare. "Boring." I dragged him there via indirect routes, including an elevator. I bet he's right. At his frenetic pace of growth, he has outgrown himself and needs some new challenge. After squabble #1 this morning, he asked me over the Cream of Wheat, "What is the future? Can I see it?" Told him only his mind could see it, that he had to close his eyes. So he did, and I began trying to drum up Anthony as a big man, Nick as a big man, Teddy as paterfamilias with kids and beloved wife.

In those days the oak table, situated as it was at the hub of our indoor activities, had become the center and symbol of family communication and sharing. It attracted and hosted the disorderly Grudin version of the tea ceremony. Its broad square surface and rich brown texture created a human space that was always inviting, always available. Its waterproof skin accommodated hot cups and chilled glasses alike. Its ample center almost cried out for a turkey or birthday cake or major salad bowl. It certainly was in part the inspiration for the scores of richly glazed cups, plates, and bowls that my wife, and soon Nick, too, turned out on the potter's wheel on the deck and fired at a local kiln. It gracefully fulfilled the purpose of all dining-room furniture: facilitating and enriching human dialogue.

But the 1990s saw a slow but inevitable family exodus. By 1996 the boys were all away at school and college, and my wife was commuting weekly to her work at Lewis and Clark College in Portland. The finish of the oak table was clouding up and softening, as though to express the irreparable encroachment of time. I stripped it and refinished it, feeling more than a bit nostalgic. I knew that it would soon be time to move on.

My adventures with furniture did not end when we sold the Eugene house and began dividing our time between Hawaii and Portland in the late 1990s. I almost killed myself during our move in 1998, when the dining-room chair I was trying to throw into the city dump bounced off a guard cable and klopped me on the head. Later that year I scoured the country shops of Multnomah and Clackamas Counties for more comfortable chairs, restoring and refinishing each that I found.

In 2004 we left the Portland house, and now, after a few years in storage, the Bakers' table sits in our dining room in Berkeley. Almost thirty-five years down the line, it still carries with it, and is ready to re-create in memory, the life and times of a young family.

The Accidental Designer

A few years ago I performed surgery on my television remote. I used a new technique, not yet approved by the American College of Surgeons, but I am glad to report that the operation went well. The patient not only survived but remains in better shape than it had been in before its accident.

Any of you who has ever dropped and broken a remote, or watched in consternation as your child dashed it to the floor or the cat knocked it off the mantelpiece, will want to know all about my surgical procedure. But before I divulge the secret, you must consider a few of the wicked thoughts that ran through my head as I did the repair. These thoughts concern the relationship between design and markets.

In some markets the durability of a household object—its ability to sustain itself in time under normal stresses—is treated as a top priority. The automobile market is a case in point. In other cases, the degree of durability is proportional to price and subject to the buyer's choice. In the power tools market, for example, a commercial-grade pressure washer can cost ten times as much as the Weekend Warrior version. "Commercial grade" means "This is a real tool."

A third type of market accepts obsolescence and trades in it. A 2004 computer may still function well, but if confronted with 2010 software, it might just as well have been driven over by a dump truck. Computer manufacturers could mitigate this obsolescence by making all components, including chip, memory, and hard drive, modular and easily replaceable through the side of the tower. That few of them have taken this relatively simple, humane, and cost-saving step has more to do with cash flow than with design principles.

A fourth type of market deliberately sets up its customers for minor but annoying disasters calculated to edify the cash register. Microsoft, for example, used to be accused of creating incompatibilities in its own Windows software with software products made by other companies and billed to be "Windows-compatible." When electronic collisions occurred, Windows would show an on-screen box with a moralistic message to the effect that the non-Windows program had performed an "illegal operation" and would now be shut down. Drop whatever you're doing, poor user. Turn out the lights; the party's over. And it's *all your fault.*

Which brings me back to my television remote. As you know, the typical remote is an oblong case with walls of light-grade plastic and only one accessible orifice: the battery compartment. The slide-out lid for this compartment typically is held in place by a tiny plastic tongue fitting into a slot in the casing wall. The fate of the entire remote rests on the survival of this little tongue. But it so happens that this fragile appendage is periodically subjected to greater stresses than any other part of the component. The reason is that AA batteries are comparatively massive. If the remote is dropped battery-side down, the batteries become much more massive: two projectiles seeking open space.

Will the renegade missiles break the poor little defenseless tongue? You can bet on it. Will the battery compartment close properly after the tongue is broken? Quoth the Raven, "Nevermore." How do missile victims deal with their tongueless tool? A tiny minority will find the part number and order another factory remote, which will cost about forty dollars and be just as vulnerable as the first. Others will try to live with a lidless battery compartment if the batteries still have a pressure fit. Others will buy a "universal" remote; they are fragile, can be hard to program, and often lack the full features of the original remote. But most will take some tape and use it to seal the batteries in.

Whatever one does, the case of the broken remote is a minor but classic example of human loss. As I sit on my futon in the wee hours, surfing from movie to movie, the naked feel of batteries against my fingers, or the feel of the sticky tape, or the feel and heft of the store-bought remote lacking my favorite buttons, makes me feel diminished, degraded. I am no longer a vested member of technological society but a disenfranchised has-been. And my big bright television set, bought only one year ago (or was it three?), begins to look like the elephant after George Orwell shot it with his rifle: suddenly very old.

And this is exactly what the people at the factory—in this case, Panasonic—must have intended. Instead of designing a durable remote control unit, as they so easily could have done, they designed an experience of loss and vexation that would ultimately drive consumers back to the shop for a new television set. The factory remote is less an instrument designed for use than a time bomb, built to break and cynically deployed in the war for market share.

How did I heal my remote? Velcro. I bought a package of four-by-two-inch Velcro pads and attached a half-inch strip of fuzzy Velcro to each side of the remote along the edge of the battery case lid. I fitted the broken lid onto the case. Then I cut a pad of non-fuzz Velcro wide enough to cover the case and attach to the fuzzy Velcro strips at each side. I stretched this pad tight so that it would give full support to the lid. Then, for a more comfortable feel, I removed the protective sheet from the Velcro pad, exposing the sticky surface, cut a fuzzy Velcro pad of the same size, and attached it to the pad in place.

You might imagine that as I went about my repair, I sang Cuban Revolution songs or muttered curses against Japanese designers. No, I just started feeling good again. When the job was done, I sat down on the futon but did not turn on the television. Sitting there, I remembered a time three decades earlier when, sick to death of television commercials, I had stormed into Radio Shack, bought a pushbutton toggle, and installed it on the lid of an old cigar box. Then I wired the toggle into the audio of my sixties-era console television, creating a hard-wired muter that I could operate with my foot when any commercial message came on.

Such experiences are rare for me. They usually begin with frustration and anger, proceed into mischievous meditation, and end with action and redemption. Do I feel redeemed by having taken revenge on corporate marketers who have been trying to exploit me? Not really. I feel redeemed by having made brief contact with my own autonomy—by having taken action in the material world.

Designing Knowledge

Professional life is essentially self-organizing. You show up at your job, work your buns off, and then come home again. If you're lucky, you're depleting your buns in hope of promotion or riches. If you're not so lucky, bun sacrifice must occur just so that you can hold on to your job. In either case, the net results are often drudgery, routine, and exhaustion.

Unless you're a college professor. Then you have long holiday breaks and whole summers free (because your students do) and, about every seven years, a sabbatical year at reduced pay. The sabbatical tradition serves the practical purpose of drawing decent people into an honorable but impecunious profession and retaining them there. It also gives them a chance to recharge their batteries. Indeed, the official rationale for sabbaticals is that they provide time for professors to make progress in their fields of expertise or even develop new areas of research and teaching.

In my case, this worked out famously. Every time I had a year off from the University of Oregon, I produced a book; and each of these books developed a new area of research. Ironically, most of these books got me into trouble with the deans, who denied me promotion as long as they could. But then, you can't have it all.

One of these sabbaticals (1978–79) is pertinent here because it taught me something about the distinction between routine and design. I had spent the previous five years in a prison of routine that ended in the award of tenure, but in the summer of 1978 I found myself not only free, but free to wander and muse in the leafy dells of the Huntington Library in San Marino, California. I decided to put in some serious dreaming. My drill was as follows: I walked out into the gardens about ten every morning, when the grounds were closed to the public. I sat quietly, let my mind wander, and occasionally scribbled something in my notebook.

These green musings gave rise to two career-changing notions. The first was that tenure had given me, technically speaking, the freedom to explore any research topic I chose. The second was that, given notion 1, I could now at least temporarily indulge my lifelong fascination with the idea of time. I quickly relaxed into my project. By next June I had filled two large notebooks with more than a thousand meditations on time.

What to do with them? It is clear from my journal that I had no idea for quite a while but that I rather enjoyed my own lack of direction:

> 11/8/78—Now about 90 entries in first draft. I have a strong wish not to see what I have already written, to tuck it behind me and completely forget it, until the whole first draft is done. I want to start each day from scratch, to carry none of the concerns of writing through the evening and into the morning. I never plan a writing day. Some days I develop a single long idea, others disparate ideas, others connected ideas. . . .
>
> I have no idea what form, if any, this book will take. Sometimes I feel that it will be treasured by readers and remembered, other times that it will flop, or, worse, that I will never get it done. But my most pervasive feeling is that what I am doing is pleasant and important to me, that it is perfect for this time in my life and for the kind of life I am living right now.

How could something so patently reckless be "perfect"? Because it made me productive. It expanded my mental scope, opening up new topics of inquiry. And it was like play. The rules of the academic game—consistency, coherent development, reliance on authority, caution—were all thrown to the wind. The project was less a demonstration, or series of demonstrations, than a continuing quest. I was seeking out the humanity of time by trying to conjure up the greatest possible variety of its manifestations. I was also seeking a voice.

In the end, the project taught me its own design. My research had acquainted me with the French Revolutionary calendar—a bold national attempt to rationalize time by going metric. Each month of this calendar was thirty days long (30 × 12 = 360), with five or six holidays added at the end of the year. By following this design I could arrange 366 sections of prose in thirteen chapters. How to organize the chapters? I had divided my notebooks into about twenty sections ("Love," "Nature," "Politics," etc.). Thirteen of these would have to do. How to spin this design to agents, publishers, and readers? The ancient "wisdom tradition" of Epictetus and Marcus Aurelius, revived by Francis Bacon in the seventeenth century and reprised in the twentieth century by Simone Weil and others, would be my excuse (it turned out to be a tough sell).

Now that the design was set, the hard work had to begin. I had to find 366 printable sections and arrange them appropriately. Over the next year and a half I selected and revised, typing each in final form on a separate sheet of paper. Then I dealt them out like playing cards.

I actually organized my book by walking around a large conference table in a vacant committee room and rearranging dozens of sheets of typing paper. This visual and physical approach to textual organization, reminiscent more of a designer's method than an author's, saved me from what would have been maddening confusion as I tried to put twelve sets, each with thirty sections, in order.

My experience with the book, published as *Time and the Art of Living,* taught me a few things about the creative process. Externally imposed designs, like my work routine before I went on sabbatical, are anathema to creativity, which thrives on the abundant wildness of free association, unlimited meditation, and unfettered exploration. I discovered that if I indulged such wildness regularly and faithfully—if I submitted myself to a regime of play and practiced the art of accident—my mind would at some point be visited by design.

This brings me back again to my earlier statement that the primary function of design is to shape and channel energy. You might say that design and energy—in this case, energy as enthusiasm, emotion, imagination—are the yin and yang of a productive life: two apparent opposites that must come into intimate dialogue with each other before a creative event can happen. Design achievements, great or small, result from episodes of focused passion.

HOMAGE TO VASARI:
DESIGN, KNOWLEDGE, AND ENERGY

Giorgio Vasari and the Permutations of Design

Sometimes thinkers make their greatest discoveries while appreciating and interpreting the genius of others. It is as though, in the very process of doing justice to the superiority of another individual, we awaken something superior in ourselves. Nothing illustrates this phenomenon so aptly as the story of the Tuscan artist and historian Giorgio Vasari (1511–74). A competent but rarely inspired painter, Vasari found his own genius in the course of memorializing the achievements of his artistic predecessors and colleagues. This effort, articulated in his great book, the *Lives* (1550, 1568), not only produced unforgettably evocative literary descriptions but provided the foundation for our modern conception of the artist and of art itself. Take, for example, Giorgio's conception of the term *design* (*disegno*) and his conclusions on Leonardo da Vinci as designer:

Design . . . is the foundation of both these arts [sculpture and painting], or rather the animating principle of all creative processes. . . .

He [Leonardo] began to practice not only one branch of the arts but all the branches in which design plays a part . . . he used to make models and plans showing how to excavate and tunnel

through mountains without difficulty . . . and he demonstrated
how to lift and draw great weights by means of levers, hoists
and winches, and ways of cleansing harbors and using pumps
to suck up water from great depths.[1]

In praising Leonardo da Vinci, Giorgio Vasari was not only recount-
ing history but also making it. In memorializing Leonardo's genius,
he laid the foundation for the modern concept of design. He did
this by expanding the meaning of the word *disegno* from a technical
description of a pictorial shape to a concept applicable to all art and
technology. The idea of design expanded in turn, coming to indicate
an inclusive knowledge base that would serve as a fulcrum for research
and speculation.

Vasari did not stop there. In 1563 he consolidated his innovative
ideas into a social institution, founding the Accademia del Disegno,
Europe's first permanent artistic establishment, in Florence. To
achieve this goal, he requested the support of the ruler of Florence,
Grand Duke Cosimo I. The duke graciously agreed and became, with
Michelangelo, the first *capo,* or honorary dean, of the new academy.[2]
Vasari's handling of this project is worth looking at, especially in
comparison with the behavior of his Japanese contemporary Sen no
Rikyu. Whereas Rikyu's resolute intensity aroused Hideyoshi's an-
tagonism, Vasari was able to convince Cosimo that cooperation with
designers was in his best interests as ruler. Rikyu played the hero;
Vasari, the diplomat. Because of Vasari's skillful approach to the
man in power, he was able to raise fine art to the status that it enjoys
today. Like Rikyu, he created a grand design for human thought and
action. Unlike Rikyu, he lived to enjoy the fruits of his labor and to
produce, in 1568, a revised edition of his magnum opus.

In the lives of both Rikyu and Vasari we see design channeling and hence liberating the flow of social energy. In both cases, moreover, we realize that the flow of energy is synonymous with the flow of knowledge. With his version of the tea ceremony, Rikyu provided a medium in which knowledge could expand; with his redefinition of design, Vasari staked out a new province of potential discovery and knowledge. In Part Two of this book I will dwell on other convergences of design and knowledge, setting forth major areas in which design principles can shape human inquiry and expression. In the chapters that follow, political and economic designs will be major objects of attention; so also will be designs in self-discipline, self-renewal, psychology, literature, the arts, and even athletics. My goal throughout will be to illustrate the unique effectiveness, as well as the necessary limitations, of design principles in the shaping of human experience.

9

The Lady in the Picture:
Design and Revelation in Renaissance Art

The hushed reverence of the gallery can fool you into believing masterpieces are polite things, visions that soothe, charm and beguile, but actually they are thugs. Merciless and wily, the greatest paintings grab you in a headlock, rough up your composure and then proceed in short order to re-arrange your sense of reality.

SIMON SCHAMA

How long can a solo artist perform without exhausting both self and audience? Two hours perhaps—three at a stretch. For artistic recognition of this fact, we need look no further than Homer's *Odyssey*. This epic poem is neatly divided into six equally long episodes—Telemachus's travels, Odysseus's arrival in the court of Alcinous, Odysseus's narrative of his journeys, and so on—each performable in two to three hours. Homer thus offers a vivid example of how physical necessity can influence the design and ultimately the meaning of art. Why, then, is the *Odyssey*, like the *Iliad*, divided into twenty-four books? Probably because when the poem was committed to writing from its original oral form, a single roll of papyrus could hold about one twenty-fourth of Homer's complete text. At that point, when the *Odyssey* was first written down, the poem might have been revised to give each "book" some structural integrity: another instance in which nature governs design, and design in turn shapes knowledge.

Homer's *Odyssey* presents a strong argument for giving the design of a work of art—its overall shaping principle—a special position in any interpretation of the work's meaning. Although sometimes, as with the *Odyssey,* design bespeaks extrinsic necessities, it can at other times reveal a subtly expressed authorial intention. Design can be used to emphasize certain elements of meaning or, conversely, to withhold information from all but the most attentive. Design can also be employed to draw beholders into a work of art and implicate them in its proceedings. Design, finally, can effectively redesign human experience to make its audience more aware of their inner nature and personal alternatives. In all of these roles, design can make art fascinating and memorable. The following examples, drawn from the Italian Renaissance, portray design functioning heroically in visual, literary, and musical art. The threads of historical influence that hold all these examples together converge in the ducal town of Mantua.

Pedro Berruguete and the Design of Knowledge

Around 1480 the young Spanish painter Pedro Berruguete made the long journey to the Italian town of Urbino to help decorate the new palace of Duke Federico da Montefeltro. The invitation to do so was not to be taken lightly. Duke Federico was the talk of Europe. The most successful of the great condottieri, a general who had never lost a single battle, he had all but single-handedly rescued Italy from Venetian domination. His leadership, a combination of wise strategy and spirited assaults, had won him the British Order of the Garter and hoards of wealth. At home, however, he was the gentlest and most peace-loving of men. He studied Aristotle under the tutelage of his close friend Maestro Lazzaro, whom he later made bishop of Urbino. Having cut his teeth at one of the first great humanist schools, Federico was an avid student of the arts and sciences who astounded academic professionals with his uncanny memory and depth of understanding. Young Berruguete had reason to be excited. He was on his way to meet a living legend.

Duke Federico was skilled in architectural design, and his new palace was without doubt his greatest work of art. His work in this line is arguably more exciting than Thomas Jefferson's, for Jefferson strove ably in the style of Palladio, whereas Federico realized an original design that became the architectural image of his own, many-faceted character. The gardens, courtyards, and balconies of his palazzo mediate between art and nature, between inner and outer space. The great building contains two chapels (one Christian, the other pagan), a set of elegant private chambers, enough spacious salons to entertain the entire town (as Federico sometimes did), and, to allow the duke to exercise his military bent, an entire floor laid out as a riding school. No building more eloquently expresses the conjoined oppositions at the heart of the humanist project: art and nature, brain and body, prowess and piety, Christianity and paganism, the public and the private. The palace was a philosophical manifesto.

Federico's greatest love, and the source of his most impassioned aspirations, was knowledge. He employed thirty to forty scribes who labored for fourteen years copying every important book he could lay hands on. Each completed manuscript was bound in scarlet and silver, except for his Bible, which merited gold. By the time of his death he had amassed the best library in Christendom. As the international bookseller Vespasiano da Bisticci put it, "A short time before the Duke went to Ferrara it chanced that I was in Urbino with his Lordship, and I had with me the catalogues of the principal Italian libraries: of the papal library, of those of S. Marco at Florence, of Pavia, and even of that of the University of Oxford, which I had procured from England. On comparing them with that of the Duke I remarked how they all failed in one respect; to wit, they possessed the same work in many examples, but lacked the other writings of the author; nor had they writers in all the faculties like this library."[1] The duke put his magnificent library at the disposal of visiting scholars, to whom he extended every courtesy.

It fell to Pedro Berruguete to paint Duke Federico's portrait (see plate). From the painting it is clear that the commission was far from simple: Federico wanted not only his likeness but his unique character memorialized for the ages. How to do this in a single frame was Pedro's challenge, and he met it as follows: The duke sits reading with his son Guidobaldo by his side. Apparently Federico has been reading aloud, for the boy's left hand is extended as though in query. Federico's book, bound in scarlet, bears on its cover his family crest. His ceremonial apron rests serenely over the full coat of armor that he is wearing; on prominent display is the Order of the Garter. A battle helmet lies on the floor to the lower right. On the lectern at the upper left, surprisingly, sits a bishop's mitre.

Berruguete's painting of the duke is a complex organization of ideas. Federico's armor suggests his martial prowess. His ceremonial garment bespeaks his public eminence, while his solitary position with his son symbolizes his private side. The bishop's mitre betokens the duke's piety—perhaps a nod to his friend Lazzaro. But the message of Berruguete's design does not stop there. The Spaniard organized his canvas into two diagonally intersecting planes:

Mitre   Federico

Book

Guidobaldo   Helmet

The opened book—symbolic of knowledge itself—thus becomes the focus of a dynamic moral geometry. It symbolically mediates between the older and younger generations and between the arts of war and those of peace. Moreover, it serves as the hub of the two diagonal lines of social energy. Berruguete thus realizes Federico's humanistic idea of knowledge as the central sustaining and renewing force in culture. By using knowledge as the focal point of his complex of symbols, the painter is able to portray not just the appearance but the philosophical character of his patron.

Giulio Romano and the Deconstruction of Design

In 1524 the reading public of Rome was variously outraged, stunned, and delighted by the worst scandal in the then brief history of printed art. A poet, Pietro Aretino, and an artist, Giulio Romano (c. 1499–1546), had teamed up with an engraver, Marcantonio Raimondi, to produce *The Ways* (*I modi*), a graphic catalog of sexual positions, each image accompanied by a naughty sonnet. *The Ways* became simultaneously a bestseller and a rare book, for the Vatican, under Pope Clement VII, was destroying every copy it could get its hands on. Raimondi was duly clapped in jail. Aretino tried to shift the blame onto Giulio, who, it turned out, had already indulged a yen for points remote. He had moved to Mantua and entered the service of Marquis (later Duke) Federico Gonzaga, that city's lord and no friend of the pope's. Marquis Federico Gonzaga was not appalled by the artist's scandal. In fact, he would exploit precisely those liberties of genius that had gotten Giulio into hot water in the first place.

Over the next decade and a half, Giulio worked on a wide variety of projects for Federico Gonzaga: everything from urban renewal to the finest art. He was especially good at producing fantastic court entertainments. In the words of Giorgio Vasari, "Nor was there ever anyone more fanciful in devising masquerades and designing extravagant costumes for jousts, festivities and tournaments, as was seen with stunned surprise by the Emperor Charles and all those who were present."[2] But Giulio's greatest achievement was a blend of architecture and painting. By 1526 he had begun the work that became the marquis' pride and joy: a massive pleasure palace outside the city where the ruler might indulge in fancies less decorous than those allowable in his urban residence. Graced with civic honors and in control of an army of artists, assistants, and laborers, Giulio spent eight years creating the Palazzo Te, a brilliantly decorated architectural tribute to pagan antiquity and sensual indulgence. Because the entire building, which stands largely intact today, was executed either by Giulio's own hand or to his express intention, the Palazzo Te can be seen as one of the largest singly designed works of art ever completed.

The palazzo is also the world's most capacious expression of the Renaissance artistic style known as mannerism. Although the term *mannerism* (from Giorgio Vasari's *maniera,* "style") has been applied to the work of artists as diverse as El Greco, Michelangelo, Cellini, Arcimboldo, Anguissola, Bruegel, Perugino, and Bronzino, it is Giulio himself who deserves pride of place for diverging from the more precise representations of his teacher Raphael and creating artistic performances that combine technical expertise with humor, self-consciousness, trickery, deliberate exaggeration, mixed genres, and fanciful conceptions. Unlike earlier Renaissance art, which was fixated on art's relation to observed nature, mannerist art could distort reality, comment on itself, invade other disciplines, and playfully enlarge on its relationship to the viewer.

Among the mannerist extremes that characterize the palace—including painting pretending to be sculpture, extravagant eroticism, and symbolic rustications—the most arresting is the Sala dei Giganti ("room of the giants"), a large chamber whose walls and ceiling double as a single panoramic painting. The painting relates, in epic style, a violent conflict between heaven and earth. From the ceiling Jupiter hurls thunderbolts down on a tribe of rebellious giants at viewers' eye-level, who are depicted being crushed under the roofs, walls, and columns of their massive quarters (see plate). There is diplomacy at work here: with the figure of Jupiter, Giulio pays tribute to Emperor Charles V, who was awed by the Palazzo Te and who consequently promoted Federico to duke. But the sala functions on three deeper levels of meaning as well, and to understand these levels is to appreciate the sophistication of Giulio's design:

First, the sala is psychologically destabilizing. Entering a room that seems to be in the process of collapse is something of a shock, especially to viewers aware that the whole palace, situated in a marsh, is not on as solid footing as it appears to be. Georgio Vasari, who had difficulty containing his rapture for the Sala, waxes eloquent on this masterpiece of trompe l'oeil: "So let no one think ever to see any work of the brush more horrible and frightening, or more realistic, than this; and whoever enters that room and sees the windows, doors and so forth all distorted and apparently hurtling down, and the mountains and buildings falling, cannot but fear that everything will crash down upon him."[3] The sala, in fact, serves as the inner sanctum of the variety of miscellaneous shocks and disorderings that make up the whole palace. The function of all these—the design goal of the Palazzo Te in general—is a displacement of sensibility, a deliberate bewilderment that separates the observer from commonsense realities and relocates awareness in a new world of fantasy and license. Nowhere more profoundly than in Giulio's palace can one sense an architecture of intoxication, a poetics of arousal. If good design tells the truth, then the Palazzo Te is telling us a profound truth about our inner energies and passions.

On a second level the sala functions as a brash political allegory. Giulio's treatment of the crumbling architecture—stone facing over brickwork—suggests that he is not thinking of the ancient days of the giants so much as of Roman architecture from Augustus down to the Christian era. Rome itself is represented by a broad-faced figure, clearly in a position of eminence. Unlike his fellows, he is clad in modern armor, and he looks skyward with his hands clasped in Christian prayer. This symbolism points to the famous sack of Rome by the forces of Charles V, an event that had occurred in 1527, the very year that Giulio began work on the palazzo. The praying figure is an effigy of Pope Clement VII, who, during the sack, had taken refuge in the Castel Sant'Angelo, itself a typical Roman construction of brick with stone facing.[4] Federico of Mantua had joined the emperor in his opposition to the pope—the same Clement who had vilified Giulio and his friends. The overthrow of the giants by Jupiter symbolizes Charles's overthrow of Clement's political authority and at the same time expresses Giulio's defense of his own artistic liberty.

This takes us to the third level of meaning, another sense in which the Sala dei Giganti constitutes a designer's declaration of independence. We would think at first that the giants' crumbling edifice is an ironic joke at the artist's own expense, implying the ultimate frailty of his or any other human handiwork. But it can also be seen as the contrary: a manifesto of artistic prowess so refined and self-conscious that it can dialogue with its own destruction. This interpretation is far more conformable to the wit, will, and conscious excess of Giulio's vision as a whole. If Pedro Berruguete's Urbino portrait is art in the service of philosophy, Giulio's Sala dei Giganti is art that overreaches philosophy in its quest for self-knowledge and expansive consciousness.

Sofonisba Anguissola and the Eye of the Beholder

The power of art to destabilize sensibility and to transfigure awareness is nowhere more evident than in a work by Sofonisba Anguissola (c. 1530–1625), the first notable woman painter of the modern world. Anguissola's illustrious career testifies to the sweeping cultural renewal of the High Renaissance. Her father, though prosperous, took the revolutionary step of having each of his daughters trained as an artist. Sofonisba he put in the care of Bernardino Campi, a noted painter who had begun his career under the influence of Giulio Romano. From early on, Sofonisba showed signs of a talent so remarkable that it drew accolades from Vasari and Michelangelo. In the 1560s she achieved international fame as court painter to Philip II of Spain, and she spent the rest of her long life enjoying affluence and renown.

The painting in question is a stunning example of mannerism at its most evocative (see plate). It is also one of the most unusual self-portraits ever realized. Sofonisba portrays herself as an image on a canvas that is being painted by none other than her own teacher, Bernardino. The teacher's face is darker, with more finely worked detail, than the face on the "canvas," which is sunnier and more sanguine: a distinction that suggests that Sofonisba is imitating Bernardino's style of portraiture for his portrait and expressing her own style for her own portrait (so, ironically, Bernardino is shown painting in his student's style).[5] Bernardino is captured in the process of detailing the brocade on Sofonisba's dress. In his left hand he holds a mahlstick pressed against the canvas to steady his right hand for this delicate work.

Bernardino is looking out to where any viewer would be standing to look at the painting, which is also where (in the pictorial fiction) the subject of his art would be sitting. Sofonisba is (from the canvas-within-a-canvas) looking at us too, as though to show that she appreciates this visual joke. She has put the viewer precisely in her own shoes.

This joke is a uniquely expressive device. By putting us in the exact position where she as model would have had to sit, Sofonisba is warping our personal space, destabilizing our own subjective paradigms and requiring us to identify with hers. Why should she want this? Look at the quiet radiance of her face. Sofonisba wants us to share her self-knowledge: to join her in celebrating her unprecedented arrival as a female art master in a world of men. In presenting herself as a painted image, she is demonstrating both her womanly beauty and her professional clout and, in the bargain, showing the kind of apparently effortless wit that, for her generation, was supposed to accompany even the most serious achievements.

Sofonisba's use of bright and dark carries its own special message. The way her face seems to cast out a light of its own in comparison to Bernardino's rather shadowy figure suggests the view, already implicit in Giulio's work, that art can generate a strange and brilliant new reality, that artistic poiesis can compete with natural creation. This view and its many ramifications reach their apogee in the next century with Shakespeare's Prospero as artist-magus in *The Tempest* and with the living statue in his *Winter's Tale,* attributed by the playwright to Giulio himself: "that rare Italian master, Julio Romano, who, had he himself eternity and could put breath into his work, would beguile Nature of her custom, so perfectly he is her ape" (V.ii.104–8).

Two other oddities in the painting deserve attention. Why would Bernardino need to look out at his subject in order to realize the minute and abstract shapes of her brocade? He ought to be focusing directly on his canvas. Has he turned his head to respond to a comment she has made or simply to appreciate her beauty? Possibly; but it is more likely that Sofonisba has turned Bernardino's face outward and fixed his eyes on the putative viewer to reinforce the viewer's identification with her as model and subject.

Finally, please follow the line of the painter's mahlstick out toward the imaginary canvas. As it crosses Sofonisba's left arm, it appears to create an indentation, as though it were pressing against real fabric. This is Sofonisba's parting shot, a play of irrepressible cleverness that reasserts the artist's capacity to subvert or reinvent our reality where and when she pleases.

Baldassare Castiglione and the Poetics of Design

What inspired Giulio Romano to alternate classic and rusticated forms and to fill the Palazzo Te with witty devices? Why did Annibale Anguissola decide to send his daughters into active professional life? What accounts for the apparently effortless wit with which Sofonisba endows her masterpiece? Barring coincidences, all these phenomena stemmed from the influence of a single book published in 1528—a book whose fame, already sweeping Italy at the time of Sofonisba's birth, soon made it the toast of Europe. This book was Baldassare Castiglione's *The Book of the Courtier* (*Il cortegiano*).

Castiglione (1478–1529) was on terms of friendship with both Federico Gonzaga and Giulio Romano. He served as Federico's ambassador to Rome, winning such praise as to earn an appointment as papal envoy to the imperial court of Charles V in 1524. But before leaving Rome he had found young Giulio a position working for Federico in Mantua. Castiglione had connections with Urbino too, having paid court to Duke Guidobaldo (Federico da Montefeltro's son, whom we saw in the portrait of his father painted by Berruguete) and his duchess, Elisabetta (Federico Gonzaga's aunt), as a young man. In a banquet hall at the Montefeltro ducal palace, with such other future notables as Pietro Bembo, Giuliano de' Medici, Ottaviano Fregoso, and Bernardo Bibbiena, he participated in a series of evening dialogues that he memorialized in his famous book. Baldassare went everywhere and knew everyone; the emperor himself eulogized him as the world's greatest gentleman. But he was also an incisive social thinker, a subtle theorist, and a grand master of Italian prose.

Published only a short time before Baldassare's death, *The Book of the Courtier* became one of the preeminent cultural artifacts of the Renaissance. Its popularity derived from its relevance, power, and scope. Though purporting to be a series of dialogues on the uses of courtiership, it is in fact a sweeping reassessment of culture, based on a thoroughly modern attitude toward politics and social behavior. In passage after passage, Castiglione champions a movement away from medieval institutions, in which culture sought stability in faith, rulebooks, and inherited authority, and toward a knowledge-based society honoring professional expertise, flexibility, and creativity. He presents human life itself as an art form in which individuals create themselves out of intuition, learning, and wit. Like Rikyu's tea ceremony, *The Book of the Courtier* is a knowledge design of epochal power in the progress of culture.

Because of his emphasis on creativity and wit as the vital components of social renewal, Castiglione can be called the godfather of

Renaissance mannerism. As the art historian Ernst Gombrich demonstrates, Giulio Romano's multiple witticisms in the Palazzo Te
—particularly his radical alternation of rough with smooth—derive
from Cicero by way of Castiglione.[6] Castiglione's celebrated formula-
tion of *sprezzatura*—making difficult feats look easy—shines forth
in Sofonisba Anguissola's radiant yet composed regard in her masterpiece of misdirection. Castiglione is also one of the precursors of
modern feminism, devoting fully one-fourth of his book to a debate
that contains virtually all the elements of feminist theory as we know
it today. When Annibale Anguissola decided to send his daughters
into the professional world as artists, he did so in a cultural climate
that was resonating with the first detailed defense of women in modern times.

An influential connoisseur of art, Castiglione took great care in
designing his own work of literature. In a manner that may have
inspired Giulio, he constructed the book architectonically, like a
building whose inner sanctum cannot be entered except through
a series of outer chambers. He presents his most harmless and least
challenging material up front (book 1 and half of book 2) and then
amuses his reader with what appears to be a mini jokebook. Book 3
contains a serious and morally charged debate on women, and book
4, in which he tackles tough philosophical issues, concludes with a
restatement of Platonic idealism. The work seems to be organized
like a modern-day college course, with the elementary material first
and the more difficult discourse later. Castiglione knew that many
readers would never get to the end of the book and that those who
did would be a self-selected group who would give his more complex
thought the consideration it deserved.

But there is an intertextual link—a kind of bridge—between the
second part of book 2 and the second part of book 4. Castiglione

had reason to fear that his opinions would be dismissed as courtly fantasies, as overly refined and revealing an ignorance of the real world. In book 4 he rebuts those who would dismiss his opinions by making Pietro Bembo zealously endorse Platonic idealism and then critiquing Bembo from a realistic perspective: "Having spoken thus far with such vehemence that he seemed almost transported and beside himself, Bembo remained silent and still, keeping his eyes turned toward heaven, as if in a daze; when Signora Emilia, who with the others had been listening to his discourse most attentively, plucked him by the hem of his robe and, shaking him a little, said, 'Take care, Messer Pietro, that with these thoughts your soul, too, does not forsake your body.'"[7] The long series of anecdotes that concludes book 2 also serves to present the evil and ignorance that constitute the dark side of humanity. Many of Castiglione's jests concern crimes committed by the church; others concern abuses of power by politicians and soldiers. His anecdotes portray a world that, for all its manifold promise, is alive with danger. By placing these jests at the end of book 2, Castiglione makes them a silent introduction to his debate on women in book 3: virtually all his anecdotes concern the failings of males.

Castiglione's placement of idealism and evil in balancing positions in his discursive design is meant not only to deflect criticism but also to suggest the moral extremes that characterize human behavior and—as extremes to be avoided—determine the course of the wise ruler. This stark contrast illustrates a philosophical statement that he makes in his own introduction: that modern times are full of ethical opposites that seem to generate each other.

The major literature of the Renaissance is full of such design strategies. Dante uses a hundred-part structure for his *Divine Comedy*. Boccaccio imitates him ironically in his bawdy *Decameron*. Machiavelli employs a symmetrical structure of twenty-seven parts in his *The Prince* to convey subtle meanings to his readers. Montaigne writes the first modern treatment of human sexual behavior and buries this X-rated item deep in his essays under the harmless title "On Some Verses of Virgil." Shakespeare sets up an elaborate three-plot structure in *The Tempest* and proceeds to set the plots off against one another like voices in a fugue.[8] Design was to Renaissance writers more or less what it was to Renaissance artists and architects: a way to focus knowledge and channel energy.

Designing an Art Form: Claudio Monteverdi

Let us return once more to Mantua. The year is 1607. Giulio is long gone, having left, in the words of his friend Vasari, an "everlasting monument" to the power of art in his many works. Among these works were his triumphs "in devising masquerades and designing extravagant costumes for jousts, festivities and tournaments." In the decades following Giulio's death, the Gonzagas' ardor for fanciful celebrations had not cooled, and at the carnival this year, before an elite organization of intellectuals, the ducal palace in Mantua rang with the sounds of something new: *Orfeo* (Orpheus), a musical drama, fittingly concerned with the power of music.

Claudio Monteverdi's *Orfeo* was the first modern opera—not the first stage work to employ sung music but the first work to integrate drama and music, speech and song, in the manner now recognized by lovers of Mozart's *The Marriage of Figaro* and *The Magic Flute*. Although the idea of such a multimedia work had been mulled over in a Florentine salon years earlier, to Monteverdi belongs the unusual distinction (shared by Joseph Haydn for his pioneering work with the symphony and the string quartet) of having designed a major art form. In later years Claudio (1567–1643) expanded on his creation with other operas, notably *The Coronation of Poppea*. His productions were internationally influential: his influence on Shakespeare's masque in *The Tempest* has been noted, and by the mid-seventeenth century, full-blooded opera would be introduced to the London stage under the guidance of Shakespeare's enterprising godson, Sir William Davenant (1606–68). Monteverdi concluded his sixty-year career famous and wealthy, the conductor of the largest musical establishment in Italy, at San Marco in Venice.

At least with Monteverdi and Mozart, opera is highly intellectual. Mozart's *Marriage of Figaro* is a subtle manifesto of social revolution, focusing on the injustice of inherited rank and the idea of human equality. His *Magic Flute* is a Masonic allegory, symbolically detailing the first steps toward true illumination. Monteverdi's audience in Mantua was the learned Accademia degli Invaghiti.[9] His artistic strategy in *Orfeo,* moreover, was both manneristic and humanistic. He held true to mannerism in that his opera, like the art of Giulio or Sofonisba, creates an engulfing world that alters the beholder's sense of self and perspective. He held true to humanism in that he created, in his opera, a learned allegory of the power of knowledge and art to allow us to engage the world on heroic terms. This allegory is buttressed by a witty *sous-conversation:* it is the composer Monteverdi himself, as well as his hero Orfeo, who is newly engaging the world with his art.

But the emotional dynamism implicit in opera could divert the form into less intellectual channels. Opera is an art form in which the power of speech and drama is fortified by vocal melodics and instrumental flair. As such, it can be more emotionally invasive than either drama without music or music without drama. Thus opera can appeal to audiences far wider than the small group of intellectuals who gathered for Monteverdi's premiere—to whole classes of people who neither read books nor look for hidden meanings in drama. Mozart was aware of this and contrived brilliantly to be a musical man for all seasons, reaching out to intellectuals and nonintellectuals alike. But those who vied for Mozart's laurels in later years, notably Richard Wagner and Giuseppe Verdi, opted for a lower road. Whatever their merits as musicians, they gave us the opera we know today: a mass-market showcase of big voices, simplistic conflicts, overblown sentimentality, and top-heavy characterizations. To say that all this is harmless fun is to err on the side of innocence. The Third Reich routinely used Wagner as a means of replacing Enlightenment rationality with Teutonic barbarism.

The Legacy of Mannerist Design

Design has always been a critical factor in art, but the mannerists, inspired by Baldassare Castiglione and Giulio Romano, opened the stops and subjected design to a variety of unprecedented uses. They pushed the envelope of esthetic experience, liberating new expressive energies and revealing new interpretive avenues. In so doing, they played a critical role in the restructuring of knowledge that would lead to the Enlightenment and modernity. The easy grace of Sofonisba's self-portrait, combined with the complex restructuring of attitudes that is the ultimate message of the painting, typifies the refined but uncompromising expansion of awareness that became the mannerist legacy.

10

In Jefferson's Footsteps:
Modes of Self-Design

In 1941, George de Mestral and his Irish pointer were hunting game birds
in the ancient Jura mountains of Switzerland. All day long, he had to pull
off sticky cockleburs clinging to the dog's coat and his own trousers.
De Mestral marvelled at the tenacity of these hitchhiking seedpods that
were difficult to disentangle from animal fur or woolen cloth.
That evening, this Swiss engineer placed a burr under a microscope and
was stunned to see that the exterior of the seedpod was covered with
masses of tiny hooks that acted like hundreds of grasping hands.
De Mestral wondered whether it would be possible to mimic nature
and create a fastener for fabric. When he succeeded he gave the creation
a memorable name by splicing together the first syllable of two
French words: *velour* (velvet) and *crochet* (hook): *Velcro.*

ALLYN FREEMAN AND BOB GOLDEN

Human beings took their first lessons in design from nature. Our
houses are hand-built metaphors for the natural shelters that we and
other animals used before the age of building. Having noticed that
wood floats, we set forth over the water in hollowed-out pieces of
wood or rafts made of bound-together tree trunks. More advanced

technical designs like stairs and the lubricated joint and the wheel took their inspirations from nature as well, as did modern wonders like the airplane and the space shuttle. We sought survival in nature by adapting its forms and exploiting its principles.

Such a vital and intimate connection between early humanity and nature suggests that human beings would continue to look to nature as a template for their own values and direction. True enough, we need only consider the primitive societies that still exist today to see evidence of such a synergy. But urban civilization took a decidedly different path. Urbanization connotes a divorce from natural principles and a reorganization of values in terms of the institutions of the state. Primary among these institutions are language, religion, and law. These institutions are profoundly normative and work together to create a new human nature: a human identity shaped not by harmony with nature but by relevance to the concerns of the state. Allegiance, patriotism, obedience, piety, and other forms of correctness are attributes that glue urban society together and prop up state authority. We can see such values in action in the Athens of 400 BC: the Athens that, within a year, executed the philosopher Socrates for "corrupting the youth."

This urban template persists to this day, in such various profusion that some form of it is evident in every modern state. Through monarchies and oligarchies, through Christianity and communism, the statist idea mooted long ago has come down to us in the present. When a US president refers to dissenters as unpatriotic, as George W. Bush did, he is trying to impose the selfsame strictures that destroyed Socrates in 399 BC. But Socrates has not remained completely silent. Voice after voice has echoed his original critique of autocracy and conformity.

Socratic dissent has a firm social and economic basis. Socrates was a realist who believed that piety, ideology, and conformity were no substitute for knowledge. This premise, advocated forcefully in turn by Plato and Aristotle, spawned the body of social thought that brought Europe into the modern world and culminated in the Enlightenment. The humanistic thesis that knowledge was the lifeblood of the commonwealth, and that its chief faculties were free inquiry, free expression, and free enterprise, sparked the revolution that gave us American democracy and liberal society. The heroes of this movement were social architects who destroyed the established templates of governance and created new forms. They designed new intellective and social worlds and, in effect, designed themselves.

Designed themselves? How are design principles brought to bear on personal affairs? Take the life of Thomas Jefferson (1743–1826): a life of repeated self-design. Son of a notably self-made man (his father, with no formal training, held high county office and served in the Virginia House of Burgesses) Jefferson set out early on to change his world. He studied law, entered the Virginia legislature, and, while still little more than a newcomer, proposed a statute abolishing slavery. In his early thirties, he played an integral part in the debates that led up to the American Revolution, and he drafted the Declaration of Independence. A few years later he composed the eloquent Statute of Virginia for Religious Freedom. As the third president of the United States, he authorized the Louisiana Purchase and, to make sure that the newly acquired land would be appreciated scientifically, sent Lewis and Clark on a long journey of discovery. He designed his two homes at Monticello and Poplar Forest, each of which bears many marks of his unique character. He not only founded the University of Virginia but designed the central buildings and established traditions that affected both the curriculum and student life. Jefferson engaged life on every level. The world spoke passionately to him, and he joined the dialogue. With a few exceptions, like Cicero and Churchill, I know of no person in history who so powerfully integrated the life of the mind with civic life.

Jefferson's designs had no template in religious principle. Although he derived his ideas from earlier thinkers, particularly Cicero, he saw himself as a radical freethinker. He endorsed the values of Freemasonry, brought to America by his esteemed friend Ben Franklin, but did not join a Masonic lodge. As he put it, "I never submitted the whole system of my opinions to the creed of any party of men whatever, in religion, in philosophy, in politics, or in anything else, where I was capable of thinking for myself. Such an addiction is the last degradation of a free and moral agent. If I could not go to heaven but with a party, I would not go there at all."[1] Jefferson did not accept the divinity of Jesus and instead took instruction from the pagan Epicurus. He respected Jesus' moral teaching but had such low regard for Matthew, Mark, Luke, and John that he neatly scissored them out of his Bible. He opined that Christianity was a good idea that had been ruined by Christians. To his mind, the three greatest modern heroes (he called them his "Trinity") were the freethinkers Bacon, Newton, and Locke. Their portraits still hang side by side prominently in his sitting room at Monticello.

In this trinity lies the secret of Jefferson's astonishing character. It is well known that he was an Enlightenment thinker, so it is no surprise that he so venerated three lions of the Enlightenment. What is sometimes forgotten, however, is that because of the likes of Bacon, Newton, and Locke, the Enlightenment itself was a direct outgrowth of Renaissance humanism. Jefferson can be described most accurately as a Renaissance man, a humanist inflamed by Enlightenment initiatives in leadership, law, science, and education. Why is it so important to see Jefferson as a humanist? Because humanistic education, more than any other way of thinking, imparts direction without imposing limit. Humanism is thus the ideal breeding ground for self-design. Humanism creates the space—perhaps the only space—where the individual can dialogue freely with the state and where truth can converse on equal terms with power.

Humanism gets a bad press these days. Marxists call it a bourgeois fantasy. Postmodernists decry it as a ruling-class dinosaur. Fundamentalists curse it as the work of the devil. Admittedly, to visit an American university campus is to find a humanism that has been ruthlessly overspecialized and overcommercialized—it is little more than the ghost of an idea. But in its heyday, from the early Renaissance up to the time of Jefferson and Goethe, humanism as a way of life was the ultimate evolutionary survival skill; humanism as an attitude toward life was a unique means of inspiring wonder and focusing energy, providing a bridge from childish frustration to personal independence.

The humanist educational strategy focused squarely on knowledge of the real world: language and human nature as revealed by history. Students learned language arts through subsets as diverse as poetry, oratory, law, philosophy, and letter writing. This concentration was not a short-term indoctrination, as in Writing 1B, but a central commitment that stretched through the student years and well beyond. Maturing students were directed into the study of history and into observation of real-world interactions. The implicit goal of this education was the reform of reigning state systems and the transformation of Europe from a set of priest-ridden medieval fiefdoms into an array of nations based on emerging conceptions of a meritocratic commonwealth. In ways that no other form of education could rival, humanism equipped Jefferson for self-sufficiency and political renewal.

What can we take from Jefferson in terms of self-design? A key lesson, I hope to show. But before going into that lesson, it may be helpful to say a word about another humanist, one as illustrious as Jefferson but somewhat less fortunate. Niccolò Machiavelli (1469–1527) was an outstanding public servant in the Republic of Florence who fell out of favor when the republic collapsed. Dismissed from civic affairs, he retired to the country. In a letter to a friend he describes his completely new life: mornings spent supervising farm projects and reading love poetry in his aviary, afternoons spent chatting and gaming at a local inn. These are ordinary enough activities, but also poignant, suggesting that the intensely gregarious Machiavelli, still in his mid-forties, is expending his social and erotic energies as best he can. But in the evenings come the really important transactions. The exile dons his old ceremonial garments and disappears into his library, where he reads the works of the ancients and, as he puts it, converses with them. From these conversations emerges Machiavelli's masterpiece, *The Prince*.

Jefferson, Machiavelli, and the Power of Example

We cannot teach somebody to be Thomas Jefferson or Niccolò Machiavelli. But we can hold up their lives to convey an attitude. Jefferson was successful in most of his major projects, but especially in those that he initiated himself. He was only twenty-six when he began designing his "dear Monticello." The experience of physically creating his own utopia must have been emotionally intoxicating. The same spirit seems to have risen in him a few years down the line when he set out to craft American liberty in the Declaration of Independence and again later in life when he built Poplar Forest and founded a university. Looking at Jefferson in detail, I find it hard to resist the inference that as a young man he discovered his own greatest strength, and indeed, the meaning of his life, in the process of design and that he projected a designer's gaze into every possible nook and cranny of experience for the rest of his life. Jefferson's example teaches us that there are few human activities as exciting or solid as imagining a project and seeing it through.

In Machiavelli we see a different aspect of the same process. Machiavelli was, at first, anything but an innovator. By all accounts, including his own, he simply loved being at the center of ongoing state affairs. He would have been happy debating, negotiating, and writing dispatches for the rest of his career, and these endeavors, if successfully continued, would have lifted him to a kind of local fame. It was professional disaster that prompted him to reassess his own life. His activities in exile were simple, regular, and pleasant. He lived what might be called intentional days. And in writing he found expression for the fierce energies that he was otherwise barred from expressing, and for the outrage that he felt toward those who had barred him. His literary projects opened up new avenues of knowledge and won him his own province of history. Because of a professional tragedy, he redesigned his life, and his resultant work renewed his spirit.

Jefferson and Machiavelli show us that design is a kind of human absolute, a form of self-fulfillment that can function with equal strength in good times and in bad. It is an engine of rationality, an angel of mercy, and a natural high.

Self-Design in the Mean Streets

Although Jefferson and Machiavelli can teach us much about attitude, they can do little to help us practice self-design in the mean streets of daily life. Most Americans, be they ever so high salaried,

are walled into narrow corridors of time by their professional obligations. The vast majority overwork to meet the goals set by their bosses,
and the bosses often feel compelled to work even harder than their
subordinates. Sought-after professions like law and medicine tend to
be the most time-consuming; to succeed, even self-employed lawyers
and doctors must become indentured servants to the calendar and
the clock. Their weekends are spent playing catch-up. They cannot
live Machiavelli's intentional day except on holiday or in retirement.
Attitudes drawn from a more leisured past may be of relevance to
them, but such attitudes are difficult to implement.

Rather than resign ourselves to lamentation, however, we should
remember that the vast US economy, which happily overworks tens
of millions of us, depends for its renewal on a smaller group of expert
professionals who are paid precisely *not* to overwork themselves but
rather to divert themselves with ideas. These are the creators of intellectual property and the consultants and professors who purvey it.
These people often work at home and often for many fewer than the
going forty-plus hours per week. Because they get paid more for the
quality of their contribution than for the quantity of their output or
the time that they take up office space, they are free to design their
own days.[2] For this reason they are free to take the Jefferson and
Machiavelli examples seriously.

But how to begin? To undertake self-design is, first of all, to re-
examine, with new seriousness, the humblest and simplest articles
of daily life. Can I increase the amount of water and sunlight in my
garden? Can it be arranged and planted to produce more abundantly?
How is my indoor living space organized? Are parts of the house conducive to conversation and friendship? Do rooms or parts of rooms
invite productive work or solitary meditation? How can I increase
convenience and reduce clutter? Is there porch space and deck space

enough to bring the outdoors in and the indoors out? Does my house call to me when I'm away and welcome me when I return? To practice self-design is to ask this new set of questions that speak less to the ways of security and success than to the ways of personal fulfillment.

A good example of how we achieve elementary self-design lies in the art of preparing food. Eating is our most intimate interface with nature. To many cultures, eating is a kind of sacrament ("God, bless this food"). Sacred or not, cooking food deliciously is an elegant performance art, and eating food with appreciation is a way of realizing and celebrating our human presence in the physical world. It can be more as well. Like other forms of design, cooking can be subtly redemptive. Without stretching the metaphor too far, let me suggest that cooking is tangible poetics, an art that brings us closer to nature and to each other.

Preparing and serving food is symbolic of self-design in general. It has all the basic components needed to renew one's world: responsibility, patience, aspiration, planning, skill, pleasure, precision, and spunk. Beginning as the expression of an inner need, it ends in outreach. People contemplating more complex initiatives of self-design—artwork, parenting, renewal of loves or friendships, intellectual breakthroughs, emotional growth—could do worse than to learn by cooking.

Learning an art like cooking can trigger psychological processes that we might call growth mechanisms. These are positive feedback loops that establish themselves when some difficult but liberating activity is learned and enjoyed and becomes integrated into a person's character. Take swimming or biking. These sports may look almost impossible at first, almost requiring a leap of faith. To learn them we must overcome fear and subdue ourselves to the counsel of experts. Yet our first moments of mastery carry a unique thrill. We are redeemed by knowledge. Our private world is a bigger place. Similarly, each growth mechanism results in an expansion of self into the outer world, making it intrinsically enjoyable.

Growth mechanisms are characteristic of youth as part of socialization and empowerment. As a teacher, I never ceased to marvel at these almost incandescent bursts of spiritual energy. The issue was how I could possibly inspire my students to experience them. I never discovered a quick and easy way. When it happened, it was sometimes because of repeated provocations, sometimes in spite of me, and sometimes for some mysterious reason. The only constant was that once the young person had activated a growth mechanism, the change was irreversible. The joy of study had become a permanent element of character.

The transfiguring power of growth mechanisms can be harnessed later in life, but only if individuals can overcome the army of myopic, retrograde, and mulish traits that usually go by the name of maturity. How many fifty-year-olds want to start law school or take up the violin? To re-experience growth mechanisms, a person must be willing to reawaken the helplessness of youth, the trusting subjection of ego, the childish confusion of contact with what is strange. Only by taking emotional risks can a person feel the energy, and appreciate the results, of real growth.

In which specific areas these redesignings of self are to occur is completely specific to the individual. I mentioned cooking as a classic art, available to almost all. Riskier and more aggressive self-design initiatives would involve addressing one's phobias and reaching into one's areas of perceived weakness. What means can be used to meet these challenges? Anything that works! Psychological issues in general are not resolved by single linear methods. The full scope of self-awareness must be brought to bear on them. Give a problem your complete attention, invite it along with you everywhere, make solving it your top priority, consult experts about it, and a variety of means, some store-bought, some homemade, will sooner or later suggest themselves.

But what of Machiavelli's intentional days? Can such a balanced and productive lifestyle be translated into contemporary practice? Begin by visualizing a good day as a sort of spiritual cocktail: a blend of the experiences we inwardly yearn for, of the actions that profoundly nourish us. When I think of such days, my mind goes back to the busiest time of my life, the 1980s and early 1990s. Weekdays I'd rise at 7:00, walk the dog, and make breakfast and bag lunches for the kids. By 9:00 I would be in my office, writing. Toward midday a bagel and an iced tea would be consumed at the computer keyboard. From 12:30 till 3:30 I would teach, hold office hours, and fulfill committee obligations. If shopping had to be done, I would do it on the way home. After that I would jog in a park near our house, often with my wife. Home again, we would cook for the kids and then relax together until storytime.

Those were happy days. Although there was nothing at all sensational about them, they humbly gave me the sustenance that I most needed. It satisfied my inner craving to care for and communicate with others, to do creative work, to engage society, to exercise physically, and to share leisure with loved ones. At root, humanity needs little more than this.

Such are the proper goals of self-design, and considering them, we may be forgiven a touch of nostalgia and a degree of hope. As modern human beings, we have come a long way from the nature that we sprang from and (early on) learned to imitate. But we have not totally lost the vital and exuberant nature that lives inside us. Until we understand this hidden treasury of energies, we cannot claim to know the full truth about ourselves. The purpose of self-design should be to regain touch with this dynamic inner nature, to live out its positive potentialities, and to bequeath it to the future.

We must also keep living nature in mind when we reshape ourselves. The wild world is full of energy, alertness, and concentration. Wild animals take their work very seriously, but they also give full attention to rest, love, and play. They engage the world with gusto. Their days are full of deeds and free of guilt. Their days are intentional in a profound sense: at once exuberant, rational, and productive. If nature cannot teach us the path of our redirection, it can suggest the spirit that we bring to our tasks.

11

Jefferson's Gravestone:
Metaphorical Extensions of Design

We meet with ideas in strange ways. In the fall of 2004, thanks to an invitation from Lynchburg College, my wife and I spent two months in the rolling hills of western Virginia. Without knowing it, we had landed in the heart of Thomas Jefferson country, only a few miles from Poplar Forest, the lesser-known of his two self-designed residences. Professor Tom Allen showed us the estate, where I became interested not only in the awkward cube-shaped room in the middle of the house but also in the most endearing structure on the property, an octagonal brick "necessary" (outhouse) that Jefferson built at a respectable, if inconvenient, remove from his abode. Soon I had visited Monticello, toured the Rotunda, quadrangle, and gardens at the University of Virginia, and ordered Merrill Peterson's collection of Jefferson's writings. Although Jefferson's creations spoke to me about many elements of design, what fascinated me most was the way his work, both architectural and literary, told me of his special character as a man.

The articulation of Jefferson's self is nowhere more apparent than in Jefferson's original gravestone, which I photographed on a brilliant November afternoon. The monument, an obelisk, is another example of Jefferson's fascination with Masonic symbols. The inscription, copied from his own last will, reads:

HERE WAS BURIED

THOMAS JEFFERSON,

AUTHOR OF THE

DECLARATION

OF

AMERICAN INDEPENDENCE

OF THE

STATUTE OF VIRGINIA

FOR RELIGIOUS FREEDOM

AND FATHER OF THE

UNIVERSITY OF VIRGINIA

These words have puzzled many visitors. Why the reference to the relatively obscure Statute of Virginia for Religious Freedom? Why no mention of Jefferson's two-term presidency or the Louisiana Purchase? The answer to these questions is probably that Jefferson, as we have seen, was at heart a designer, and his own designs, including his public writings and the university he founded, were dearest to him.[1] Beyond this, moreover, he projected elements of design into his political life. Let's look briefly at his Declaration of Independence and his Statute of Virginia for Religious Freedom from a designer's perspective.

Both the declaration and the statute are examples of literary design, drawing their inspiration from rhetorical principles firmly established in antiquity and the Renaissance. Jefferson's favorite verbal instrument in both works is the device known as *copia,* which normally consists of an eloquent piling up of diverse details that all relate to a central topic or theme. His use of copia derives from the Roman statesman Cicero, whom Jefferson admired so much that he called him the "first master of the world." In the Declaration of Independence, Jefferson employs copia to characterize the injustices of the king in a series of accusatory sentences:

He has refused his Assent to Laws, the most wholesome and necessary for the public good.

He has forbidden his Governors to pass Laws of immediate and pressing importance, unless suspended in their operation till his Assent should be obtained; and when so suspended, he has utterly neglected to attend to them.

He has refused to pass other Laws for the accommodation of large districts of people, unless those people would relinquish the right of Representation in the Legislature, a right inestimable to them and formidable to tyrants only.

He has called together legislative bodies at places unusual, uncomfortable, and distant from the depository of their public Records, for the sole purpose of fatiguing them into compliance with his measures.

He has dissolved Representative Houses repeatedly, for opposing with manly firmness his invasions on the rights of the people. . . .[2]

In his statute (also known as the Bill for Establishing Religious Freedom) he loads his whole case for religious freedom into a behemoth of a sentence, a copia of clauses so accumulative, so overwhelming, that it would seem to defy contradiction. I quote only a part:

. . . that to compel a man to furnish contributions of money for the propagation of opinions which he disbelieves and abhors, is sinful and tyrannical; that even the forcing him to support this or that teacher of his own religious persuasion, is depriving him of the comfortable liberty of giving his contributions to the particular pastor whose morals he would make his pattern, and whose powers he feels most persuasive to righteousness; and is withdrawing from the ministry those temporary rewards, which proceeding from an approbation of their personal conduct, are an additional incitement to earnest and unremitting labours for the instruction of mankind; that our civil rights have no dependence on our religious opinions, any more than our opinions in physics or geometry; that therefore the proscribing any citizen as unworthy the public confidence by laying upon him an incapacity of being called to offices of trust and emolument, unless he profess or renounce this or that religious opinion, is depriving him injuriously of those privileges and advantages to which, in common with his fellow citizens, he has a natural right; that it tends also to corrupt the principles of that very religion it is meant to encourage, by bribing, with a monopoly of worldly honours and emoluments, those who will externally profess and conform to it; that though indeed these are criminals who do not withstand such temptation, yet neither are those innocent who lay the bait in their way; that the opinions of men are not the object of civil government, nor under its jurisdiction; that to suffer the civil magistrate to intrude his powers into the field of opinion and to restrain the profession or propagation of principles on supposition of their ill tendency is a dangerous fallacy, which at once destroys all religious liberty, because he being of course judge of that tendency will make his opinions the rule of judgment, and approve or condemn the sentiments of others only as they shall square with or differ from his own; that it is time enough for the rightful purposes of civil government for its officers to interfere when principles break out into overt acts against peace and good order; and finally, that truth is great and will prevail if left to herself; that she is the proper and sufficient antagonist to error, and has nothing to fear from the conflict unless by human interposition disarmed of her natural weapons, free argument and debate; errors ceasing to be dangerous when it is permitted freely to contradict them.

Jefferson's prose style reflects the mind of a designer. Because he understood that a major design of any sort must, insofar as possible, live and breathe like the world around it, he built into the statute not just one or two telling points but a veritable city of language in which every phrase engages reality from a different but equally valid perspective. He understood that a work's vitality depends on its details, but that details are useless unless they build a coherent whole. And he understood that *that* whole, no matter how impressive its internal dynamics, cannot function well or long unless it is designed to engage the full continuum of political experience.[3] It is designs of this sort that democracies depend on. The declaration and the statute are designs for liberty; in a metaphorical sense, so is the third of his favorite achievements, the University of Virginia.[4]

"A metaphorical sense." We have already seen that design as a metaphor can shed light on several of life's crucial issues. Let us leave Jefferson briefly and look further into the metaphor's various uses. Take the popular term *social design* as defined by Langdon Morris: "The term 'social design' therefore refers to that aspect of architecture which takes as a priority the creation of environments for effective and positive human interaction, and in the end asks the question: Can better buildings make for a better quality of interaction?"[5] Social design extends design principles into areas like knowledge management. Other researchers and consultants explore organizational design, educational design, research design, motivational design, and other professional ramifications of the subject, as well as more homespun specialties like vacation design, honeymoon design, and designer eggs.

What gives the word *design* such cachet? The word is richer in meaning than its straiter-laced competitors, *planning* and *theory*. *Design* suggests real-world substance and real-world use; it suggests three-dimensionality and mass. Good designers know the materials they work with; they consider the good of the user; they think holistically; they reshape the world. Metaphorically, then, *design* carries connotations of liberty, advanced consciousness, attention to reality, enhanced power, and solid skill.

No practitioner of design is more attentive to these connotations than Matt Taylor, co-developer (with his wife Gail) of Group Genius, DesignShop, and other innovative consulting techniques. The Taylors, whose clients and collaborators have included NASA, the Wharton School, the US military, and the World Economic Forum, have integrated concepts of good design into all of their corporate activities. They have designed or redesigned their meeting-places from the ground up. They have created a whole new vocabulary for conferencing processes. Using these and other means, they have taught their clients to think like designers—not so much designers of things as designers of their own futures. In so doing, the Taylors have (in their own words) "compressed time": that is, shortened the amount of time necessary for organizational innovation. As the DesignShop executive Todd Johnston puts it, their strategy enables "groups of as few as ten or as many as several hundred to design together solutions to complex organizational issues in a fraction of the time of traditional business planning or design processes. This methodology evokes what the Taylors call 'Group Genius': The ability of a group working consistently and collaboratively to seek, model and put into place higher-order solutions. Design is often thought of as an individual activity/discipline. I think it is notable that the design the Taylors 'teach' and the process they've invented is for people to be able to design together. In their work with organizations, the knowledge transfer extends far beyond the executive offices, to every corner of the organization, emphasizing design as a way of working top-down and bottom-up simultaneously."[6] The Taylors' methodology suggests the influence of three twentieth-century innovations: creativity theory as ushered in by Carl Rogers and Rollo May, Friedrich von Hayek's idea of a knowledge-based economy, and the proactive design concepts of Matt Taylor's teacher, Frank Lloyd Wright. To these they have added numerous refinements of their own, including a novel blending of the hypothetical method and the thought experiment ("What if?"). Their work represents to me one of the most extreme permutations of design into the world at large.

While thinking about the Taylors I discovered that I myself had long been using a kind of designer strategy in advising college undergraduates. If juniors or seniors expressed uncertainty about life after graduation, I would ask them to look into the future and sketch for themselves the kind of life they would like to be living at age fifty. Without asking them to name a specific profession, I would sketch broad alternatives, such as whether they would like to be working solo, like an artist, or professionally, like a lawyer, or in a social or corporate setting. I would ask whether they saw themselves living in an urban setting or not, whether they would have families, and what sort of professional relationships with people they would have developed. In this way I challenged them to design, if only for an hour, a future life.

Design and Leadership: Theodore Roosevelt
and Augustus Caesar

It requires no great leap of understanding to see that the same design principles that can operate in an individual's life can also apply, via sound leadership, to large-scale social evolutions. Indeed, sound leadership itself is based on the ability to design some future good and focus social attention on achieving it. Probably the most dramatic example of design in presidential politics is found in the tenure of Theodore Roosevelt. As an unelected president (he succeeded William McKinley after the latter's assassination), he took office without a popular mandate but soon embarked on policies so considered and so coherent that they amounted to an economic makeover of the nation. During his first term he broke the corporate trusts that were threatening America's democratic traditions. After reelection he invigorated the Interstate Commerce Commission and other consumer-protection agencies and set aside 194,000,000 acres of land for national parks (about 450 percent more than all of his predecessors combined). These and other achievements revolutionized the national infrastructure in ways that consistently protected American land and liberty. Roosevelt redesigned and redirected American democracy, provoking the scholar Harvey Mansfield to comment that Roosevelt's strategies were like William James's idea of the "moral equivalent of war" and inviting comparisons with wartime presidents Abraham Lincoln and (Theodore's cousin) Franklin Delano Roosevelt.[7]

Teddy Roosevelt's major enemy, as he later realized, was time. Had he run for and won a consecutive third term, he might have taken the United States much further along the lines that he had charted. To find a progressive leader who followed design principles without severe time constraints, we must look beyond the American system and back to ancient Rome. Gaius Octavius, later known as Augustus Caesar, led Rome for almost sixty years, during which time he devoted himself to a series of vast reforms and innovations that were all of a piece. In his own words,

> I raised an army with which I set free the state, which was oppressed by the domination of a faction. . . . I drove the men who slaughtered my father into exile with a legal order, punishing their crime, and afterwards, when they waged war on the state, I conquered them in two battles. I often waged war, civil and foreign, on the earth and sea, in the whole wide world, and as victor I spared all the citizens who sought pardon. As for foreign nations, those which I was able to safely forgive, I preferred to preserve than to destroy. About five hundred thousand Roman citizens were sworn to me. I led something more than three hundred thousand of them into colonies and I returned them to their cities, after their stipend had been earned, and I assigned all of them fields or gave them money for their military service. . . . I paid the towns money for the fields which I had assigned to soldiers. . . . I restored peace to the sea from pirates. . . . I extended the borders of all the provinces of the Roman people which neighbored nations not subject to our rule. . . . I added Egypt to the rule of the Roman people. . . . I founded colonies of soldiers in Africa, Sicily, Macedonia, each Spain, Greece, Asia, Syria, Narbonian Gaul, and Pisidia.[8]

We cannot take these claims (published in Rome on bronze columns) without a grain of salt. Augustus omits Mark Antony's pivotal role in the war against Brutus and Cassius and understates the accomplishments of his brilliant colleague Marcus Agrippa. But his other claims are justified, and together they amount to what is probably the greatest project of social renewal ever achieved by a single leader. Augustus found Rome in pieces and reunited it. He turned the Mediterranean Sea into a Roman lake, bringing the whole region under the influence of a relatively enlightened culture. His social programs were little short of visionary. He enriched his lands and colonies with trade and enterprise. In short, he took a nation that was at the brink of chaos and built it into a coherent empire, united under the rule of reason.

"Built it": that is key. The whole concept of construction was almost sacred in Augustan Rome, whose vocabulary had at least seven different words for the process. Here is Augustus describing his own building projects:

> I built the senate-house and the Chalcidicum which adjoins it and the temple of Apollo on the Palatine with porticos, the temple of divine Julius, the Lupercal, the portico at the Flaminian circus, which I allowed to be called by the name Octavian, after he who had earlier built in the same place, the state box at the great circus, the temple on the Capitoline of Jupiter Subduer and Jupiter Thunderer, the temple of Quirinus, the temples of Minerva and Queen Juno and Jupiter Liberator on the Aventine, the temple of the Lares at the top of the holy street, the temple of the gods of the Penates on the Velian, the temple of Youth, and the temple of the Great Mother on the Palatine, etc.[9]

In addition, Augustus reminds the world that he rebuilt the theater of Pompey, rebuilt numerous aqueducts, and completed the Forum of Julius and its basilica. Augustus lavishes more detail on his role as public architect than on any of his other achievements. As a builder, he was honored by the acknowledged father of architectural theory, Vitruvius, who saw public design as the proper extension of political power and who expressed the wish that "not only should the state have been enriched with provinces by your means, but that the greatness of its power might likewise be attended with distinguished authority in its public buildings."[10]

Augustus—like his great-uncle and adoptive father, Julius Caesar, before him, and like his illustrious successors Trajan and Hadrian—performed as an urban designer as well as a leader. This tradition of design and policy was not lost on Thomas Jefferson, who studied the ancient Romans and realized their architectural ideas in brick and plaster.

The idea of design enlivened Augustan politics in less material ways. Augustus always had multiple public projects afoot that involved his citizens in activities at once sane and constructive. He kept countless Romans too busy to grumble and made them into architects of their own commonwealth and their own urban dignity. Indeed, Augustan design shows a political strategy of vision: a vision of Rome as a construct eternally in the making. Each achievement prepared the way for another. Augustus remained a popular figure throughout, and in the end he was able to resign as emperor without any loss of influence or public respect: "In my sixth and seventh consulates, after putting out the civil war, having obtained all things by universal consent, I handed over the state from my power to the dominion of the senate and Roman people. . . . After that time, I exceeded all in influence, but I had no greater power than the others who were colleagues with me in each magistracy."[11]

The emperor had built well. After his death in AD 14, the Roman polity survived the reigns of several lesser leaders, including reprobates like Caligula and Nero, until it was rescued by Nerva eight decades later.

The long and vigorous tenure of Augustus suggests to us that design principles give motivation and coherence to leadership. It is not too much to say that all leaders should always keep the future designs of their organizations in mind and use the spirit of design to animate the positive energies of their subordinates.

The Origin of Design as a Concept

Appropriately, we get our noun and verb *design* from a Latin root. *Designare* was a workhorse of a word with manifold meanings: "mark; point/mark/trace out, outline/describe; indicate/designate/denote; earmark/choose; appoint, elect (magistrate); order/plan; scheme; perpetrate." This little crowd of meanings suggests the character of the Augustan spirit: practical, systematic, dominating, yet also curiously creative. The Roman passion for design animated public works well into the second century AD; but in succeeding centuries, as Roman culture declined and Christianity advanced, design and other art-related ideas fell into disuse.

Not totally, however. The Roman *collegium* (union) of architects was allowed to survive, at least vestigially, through the Middle Ages and into the Renaissance, probably as a means of facilitating large-scale construction. To this brotherhood of skilled professionals fell the task of constructing cathedrals and other public works. Working under the aegis of the powerful Knights Templar in thirteenth-century Paris, those in the fellowship of masons were granted the advantages of *franc-métiers:* freedom from feudal obligations and freedom to travel. The title Freemasons first appeared in fourteenth-century England. Composed in the main of master architects and their apprentices, the Freemasons were a dignified order of men who, with some justification, could view themselves as the intellectual superiors of most of their contemporaries. They met to discuss their craft at what came to be known as lodges. Gradually their discussions grew more speculative, and their meetings began to include visits by experts who had nothing specifically to do with architecture. In the seventeenth and eighteenth centuries the organization evolved into a freethinking society that wielded broad influence in England and America, especially in the age of Franklin and Jefferson.[12]

As we have already seen, however, our modern concept of design as a field of study arose from a different source. Giorgio Vasari was important not only for introducing this concept of design but for other reasons as well. He created, in large measure, the modern discourse of art history and art appreciation. Moreover, his narratives elevated artists like Giulio Romano and Michelangelo from their earlier positions as skilled technicians—the young Michelangelo was punished by his family for his love of art—to places of heroic stature at the center of a society that they renewed with their genius. For this revolutionary purpose he fittingly characterized design as divinely born and divinely inspired. Largely thanks to Vasari, Western artists took on importance as cultural icons, and with this importance came the license to range further and further afield in style and subject matter.[13]

But Vasari's idea of design as a discipline-transcending process did not come of age professionally for three more centuries. The firm of Morris, Marshall, Faulkner and Company, established in London in 1861, was the first organization with all the earmarks of a modern design consultancy, and its founder, William Morris (1834–96), is usually the first to be mentioned in histories of design as a profession. A poet, social thinker, publisher, and theorist, Morris was also a pioneer in the development of interior design. He rejected the miscellaneously decorated interiors in vogue among the Victorians and instead created integrated interiors in which the furniture and the decorations shared the same visual thematics as the room at large. In this cause he personally produced many captivating designs in textiles, carpets, wallpaper, stained glass, and furniture. Writing much and lecturing widely on topics that ranged from the practical to the utopian, Morris brought a unified character to the design profession and raised design to the level of a fine art.

At the turn of the twentieth century, designers still had one more question to tackle: mass production. Would design remain the treasure of a few elite clients, or could it be transmitted to the world at large? The United States provided the answer to that question in the person of Frank Alvah Parsons (1866–1930). In 1910, Parsons became president of the Chase School in New York (later to bear his name), and over the next twenty years he turned it into the first modern school of design. He extended the scope of design to include mass-produced items, which brought design to center stage in the modern world. To quote from the school's Web site: "By locating visual beauty in the ordinary things of middle-class American life, Parsons virtually invented the modern concept of design in America. From the beginning, the faculty cared about the spaces people lived in, the garments they wore, the advertising they read, the furniture and tableware they used. The principles they taught had the effect of democratizing taste and making it available to America on a broad scale."[14]

By the 1930s design had become a recognized professional area, with specialties like fashion design and interior design being taught at the Parsons School. By this time, parallel principles were at work in the Bauhaus school in Weimar, Germany. The Bauhaus style had grown out of the achievements of the Belgian Henri van de Velde, who, under the influence of Morris, had been one of the founders of art nouveau.

The history of the idea of design suggests the dignity and promise of the calling. From the time that Vasari introduced the idea of design, its practitioners—people like Augustus, Jefferson, and Roosevelt—have extended it, producing works that suggest its rich and powerful ramifications. Design is a kind of magical idea. Unlike any other concept, it calls for us to create a unity of part with whole, a concord of form and function, a finished product that is harmonious with society and with nature. Design is a provocative metaphor for creative thought in any area at all.

The Limits of Design: William Blake

No study of design as metaphor can do without a look at Thomas Jefferson's celebrated British contemporary the poet William Blake (1757–1827). Blake holds a special position in English esthetic history, but not by virtue of literary achievement alone. With a few welcome exceptions he was at best an able lyricist, at worst a tedious merchandiser of words about angels. His thought was unfocused, without weight, wit, or drama. He lacked the essential ingredient of poetic greatness: an alertness to physical immediacy. In fact, his mind was elsewhere. As his wife once put it, "I have very little of Mr. Blake's company. He is always in Paradise."

What so endears Blake to readers is the extent and coherence of his esthetic conviction. A better illustrator than he was poet, he decorated his verses with graphics so apt and eloquent that they radically enhanced the meaning of his words. He thus created a mixed genre in which the whole was indeed greater than the sum of its parts. But Blake did not stop there. He personally engraved, printed, and colored his pages, overseeing the progress of his books from inspiration to sale. His production process was nothing if not laborious. Picking up a copper printing plate, he beveled its edges and polished it to mirror-like smoothness. Then he covered the plate with a varnish made of beeswax and asphaltum and blackened its surface with candle smoke. "Once the varnish was hardened and blackened, Blake's design could then be drawn on the varnished plate. Blake could either compose directly onto the plate or copy from an original design drawn on paper. Once the image was reduced from the original to fit the plate size, it had to be transferred directly to the plate. Blake then transferred the drawing with a blunt and round-pointed needle called a stift or calking needle, thus depositing on the plate particles of chalk along every line in the original design. Because calking reverses right to left in a print taken from the plate, the preliminary drawing had to be counterproved—transferred in reverse—onto the plate face down. Actual etching could begin."[15] Blake then added acid to bite the plate—a process that alone took about nine hours. After cleaning, the plate was ready to print. Blake covered it with intaglio ink and pressed it to the page. He later added any coloring by hand.

This grueling and tedious process gave Blake complete control over production. His books emerged as organic extensions of his own personality. His meaning is not imprisoned in his words but rather is an offspring of the marriage between words and design. Even for one who cannot share his faith or praise his verse, it is difficult to look at a page of his without a sense of veneration for someone who profoundly embodied the human propensity for design.

An anecdote speaks both to Blake's eccentricity and to his integrity: "One day a visitor surprised William Blake while he was working alone on a picture in his studio. His guest was astonished to discover that he was apparently working on a portrait—of an invisible sitter: he looked and drew, and looked and drew, apparently intent on capturing the spirit's likeness. When the visitor attempted to speak, Blake interrupted him. 'Do not disturb me,' he pleaded. 'I have one sitting to me.' 'But there's no one here,' the man replied. 'But I see him, sir,' Blake insisted. 'There he is; his name is Lot—you may read of him in the Scriptures. He is sitting for his portrait.'"[16] Whatever our opinion of Blake's rationality, his vision of Lot proves that for him, design was a single unbroken process from conception to printed page.

The Scope and Dignity of Design

Jefferson, Roosevelt, Augustus, and Blake all belong to a special category of designers: those who personally bring their designs to completion. Their lives illustrate the scope and dignity implicit in the process of design. They suggest forcefully that while deeds of valor, rushes of genius, and the whole human gallery of triumphs, adventures, and ordeals may have greater shock value, nothing can really match the humble project of hatching an idea and developing it to fruition. Such projects, especially when they concern social issues, draw designers out of the ranks of specialists and place them in the full theater of humanity.

Liberty as a Knowledge Design

I hope we shall crush in its birth the aristocracy of our monied
corporations which dare already to challenge our government to
a trial by strength, and bid defiance to the laws of our country.

THOMAS JEFFERSON

I do most anxiously wish to see the highest degrees of education given
to the higher degrees of genius and to all degrees of it, so much as may
enable them to read and understand what is going on in the world
and to keep their part of it going on right; for nothing can keep it right
but their own vigilant and distrustful superintendence.

THOMAS JEFFERSON

When, after six years of struggle, George Washington succeeded
in leading the American colonies to victory as a nation free of the
English monarchy, a vocal contingent of fellow colonists suggested
that Washington be crowned king of the United States. This ironic
incident suggests the sad truth that liberty, the hardest political goal
to achieve, is also the treasure most easily lost or thrown away.

We need not look far to see why. Unlike other forms of government, democracies are run by the people; and the people's greatest

weakness is its tendency to devalue liberty in favor of wealth and security. America's notorious complacency, enshrined in a degraded educational system and pandered to by the media, is one symptom of this devaluation. Another is the rise to hegemony of American corporations, those insatiable seekers after wealth, which erode American liberty by indulging in self-interested lobbying. These corporations assert that they are exercising liberty, but if so, it is not the liberty that Thomas Jefferson envisaged. To Jefferson and his colleagues, American liberty was a complex assortment of attitudes, instilled by culture, enshrined in literature, alive in language, and embodied in the individual. To corporations and their Washington, DC, supporters, on the other hand, liberty is little more than a piggybank and a permissive marketplace.

This superficial and self-serving definition of liberty becomes especially dangerous when it leads to the assumption that democracy can be exported abroad, much the way Virginia exports hams. We have seen the fruits of this attitude in US policy toward Iraq. President George W. Bush's plan for Iraq boiled down to two major elements: the forcible ouster of Saddam Hussein and the construction of democratic government. But the plan flew in the face of reality. Destroying Saddam's power structure may have looked good on paper, but it gave rise to as many evils as it alleviated. The Bush-Rumsfeld plan for Iraq ignored the division between the Sunni and Shi'ite branches of Islam, the basis of the largest political confrontation in that country today. It ignored the presence of a politicized form of Islamic fundamentalism that refuses to recognize the separation of church and state that the West considers indispensable to democracy. And it ignored the lack of institutions and social structures of democracy in Iraq—what Tocqueville called the requisite "habits of the heart."

It is largely because these habits of the heart are lacking that not a single Arab state has ever completely evolved into a democracy. At best, in Turkey and Egypt, Islam remains a powerful player in a none-too-stable coalition with secular government. At worst, as in Iran, Islam reigns absolute. Islam is profoundly political. As the Iranian strongman Ayatollah Khomeini put it, Islam is politics itself. This infrastructural barrier to democracy was, it seems, completely ignored by the American planners who sought to design a democracy for Iraq. We know from the US Constitution and the constitutions of other free states that the conditions of liberty *can* be designed, but not without the cultural raw material necessary for its existence.

These circumstances raise a number of questions. What was the complex assortment of attitudes that made up the Founders' idea of liberty, and how did it evolve? Is American liberty, as currently enjoyed, sustainable even in America? Are alternative versions of liberty available to non-Western states? Let me touch on these questions in order:

What was the complex assortment of attitudes that made up the Founders' idea of liberty, and how did it evolve?

In the preceding chapter I quoted part of the colossal sentence that forms the backbone of Jefferson's Statute of Virginia for Religious Freedom. Largely because this sentence was based on a rhetorical blueprint from ancient Rome, I called it a literary design. It is, in fact, much more than this. In his effort to exhaust the valid implications of an idea, Jefferson created a knowledge design: an outline that, with the character of a detailed anatomical study, would suggest the idea of human liberty. For liberty, as Jefferson understood it, was not just a legal prerogative, not just a privileged way of life. It was an intrinsically literate sense of right and responsibility. Jeffersonian liberty was a body of knowledge.

By Jefferson's time, this knowledge design had been a millennium in the making. It had its origins in the revival of ancient Greek thought in various parts of the Arab world from the ninth to the twelfth centuries. Its point of departure, ironically, was the once-magnificent city of Baghdad, under the Abassid caliphate. An Arab historian describes one caliph, Mamun (786–833), as a humanist of the highest order:

He looked for knowledge where it was evident, and thanks to the breadth of his conceptions and the power of his intelligence, he drew it from places where it was hidden. He entered into relations with the emperors of Byzantium, gave them rich gifts, and asked them to give him books of philosophy which they had in their possession. These emperors sent him those works of Plato, Aristotle, Hippocrates, Galen, Euclid, and Ptolemy which they had. Mamun then chose the most experienced translators and commissioned them to translate these works to the best of their ability. After the translating was done as perfectly as possible, the caliph urged his subjects to read the translations and encouraged them to study them. Consequently, the scientific movement became stronger under this prince's reign. Scholars held high rank, and the caliph surrounded himself with learned men, legal experts, traditionalists, rationalists, theologians, lexicographers, annalists, metricians, and genealogists.[1]

Mamun was patron to the first great Arab Aristotelian, Abu Yousuf Yaqub ibn Ishaq al-Kindi (805–73), who composed the following epochal endorsement of free thought: "We ought not to be embarrassed of appreciating the truth and of obtaining it wherever it comes from, even if it comes from races distant and nations different from us. Nothing should be dearer to the seeker of truth than the truth itself, and there is no deterioration of the truth, nor belittling either of one who speaks it or conveys it."[2]

Although Arab cultural achievements would be dealt a serious blow by the Mongol invasion of 1258, succeeding generations saw major scientific progress, the rise of Arabic poetry, the great age of the Muslim fresco, the international preeminence of Arab medicine, major advances in manufacture and trade, the brilliant historiography of Ibn Khaldun (1332–1406), and the spectacular court of Suleyman the Magnificent (1494–1566) in Istanbul. The history of modern Islam is not a case of a culture that never progressed. It is the story of a culture that achieved a precocious level of illumination and then mostly renounced it in the name of fundamentalist authority.[3]

But the renaissance that was ultimately forsaken by the Arabs found a permanent home in Europe. The conduit for the flow of ideas was Spain. Averroes (Ibn Rushd, 1126–98), a Spanish Arab intellectual beneficiary of the philosophical tradition that had commenced in Baghdad and included Al-Kindi, Avicenna, Al-Farabi, and Avempace, produced a series of commentaries on Aristotle. He also developed a manifesto, later referred to as the double truth, in which he decorously argued that religious faith and scientific inquiry could jointly prosper. But couched within this argument was the radical notion of intellectual freedom. The history of our freedom today began with an Arab's endorsement of free thought.

During the century after Averroes' death, Aristotelian thinking spread rapidly, making its influence felt in the imperial court of Frederick II, the court of Alphonso the Wise in Castile, and the University of Paris. In the mid-thirteenth century it drew the attention of a Florentine thinker and statesman named Brunetto Latini (c. 1220–94), who, in turn, conveyed it meaningfully to one of his students, the young Dante Alighieri (1265–1321). Years later, in exile, Dante used

Aristotelian methodology in arguing against the papal domination of Europe (*On Monarchy*).[4] Granted, Dante was at this point writing as a monarchist, but his book nonetheless laid the groundwork for a second major component of liberty, the separation of church and state.

Educating Dante was by no means Brunetto's most memorable achievement. In his own time he was credited with reeducating the whole Florentine commune. In the process, he created a literary and civic fulcrum for the development of modern political thought. Brunetto saw that Florence could never achieve autonomy if its culture remained under the domination of feudal values and ecclesiastical authority. To counter these forces he created his own massive knowledge design: a learned and eloquent book that he aptly titled *The Treasure*. Brunetto's treasure was no less than the handbook for a new culture. The book's three main components—Aristotelian ethics, Ciceronian oratory, and statesmanly precepts culled from the author's experiences at home and abroad—combined to form an educational program that would free his readers to take civic action in a representative and self-sustaining government. *The Treasure* was quickly and massively influential. Together with Brunetto's other writings and his actions as a civic leader, it influenced the development of Florentine culture for generations to come. Brunetto was thus the effective founder of the intellectual and political program that we have come to know as humanism. In the hands of later spokesmen like Francesco Petrarca, Giovanni Boccaccio, and Coluccio Salutati, this humanistic discourse sustained the revolution that created the Renaissance.

Brunetto's work liberated his fellow Florentines. Appropriately they soon came to describe their government with the Latin word *libertas*.[5] This word became their battle cry in times of stress, especially when the city went to war against the Avignon papacy in 1375. *Libertas* persists as a Florentine motto to this day. Although Florentine libertas did not survive the end of the fifteenth century, it exerted a deep influence on Niccolò Machiavelli, who broadcast the idea to the modern world.

To find four major components of liberty (free thought, separation of church and state, representative government, and the idea of liberty) affecting a single city within a single century is to understand how contagious, how inebriating, the idea of freedom is. It is also to understand why liberty, and its implications for human behavior, persisted unflaggingly in the thematics of that characteristically Florentine masterpiece Boccaccio's *Decameron* (1349–72). Boccaccio's book begins with a symbolic liberation: Ten young aristocrats leave the city of Florence, where plague has introduced all forms of corruption, and sally forth to a series of villas that reflect in all ways the delights of art and nature. The young people establish their own intellectual republic, which observes rules of free expression and strict equality, and begin swapping yarns. Before they go home, they have related one hundred stories, in each of which some moral aperçu is wrapped up in narrative. The morality of the *Decameron* is persistently liberating. Read with attention, Boccaccio's book is a bible of modern liberty.

The morality of the *Decameron* amounts to a humanist rejection of medieval authority. Boccaccio gives precedence to reason and nature over their Christian counterparts, faith and God. His characters speak out for women's rights, and one of his main figures declares bluntly, for the first time in the modern world, that all human beings are created equal.[6] Great emphasis is placed on knowledge, awareness, and eloquence, insofar as these qualities can lead to effective action in society. The *Decameron* is the first comprehensive literary statement of the humanist vision introduced in Florence by Brunetto. Over the years to come, the humanist program would be reiterated in countless forms, eventually animating the mind of Thomas Jefferson.

Similarly revolutionary attitudes expressed themselves in Renaissance art, philosophy, and science. Around 1440, Donatello produced the first freestanding nude sculpture (his *David*) seen in Europe since pagan antiquity. His initiative gave rise to a wave of European art lionizing the naked human form and asserting the viewer's right to enjoy it. Giorgio Vasari, as we have seen, proclaimed art itself to be a heroic activity—above all, that art which moved beyond the mere representation of reality into the realm of fantasy and invention. Desiderius Erasmus (1466–1536) introduced the theme of diversity (copia again) into the history of ideas. Niccolò Machiavelli promoted civil liberties in his *Discourses* and produced, in *The Prince* (written in 1513), the first unabashedly modern account of the political arena. Baldassare Castiglione's *The Courtier* (1528) provided a template for the skills necessary in such an arena. Michel de Montaigne (1533–92) established self-inquiry as a serious step in the quest for knowledge. Francis Bacon (1561–1626) codified, in large measure, the principles of modern science. All of these actions dramatically increased the scope of human expression and inquiry and hence contributed to the modern idea of liberty.

By the mid-seventeenth century the other major components of liberty had been introduced. Montaigne's friend Étienne de la Boétie (1530–63) announced, in his *Discourse on Voluntary Servitude,* that all human beings are born into liberty, and laid the groundwork for the modern idea of civil rights. The statesman William the Silent (1533–84) championed religious tolerance. John Milton (1608–74) wrote a bold defense of free speech (*Areopagitica*) and, along with Roger Williams (c. 1603–c. 1684), was a forceful advocate for religious freedom. Benedict Spinoza (1632–77) built liberal democracy into his epoch-making treatise, the *Ethics*. The Moravian "Teacher of Nations," Jan Amos Comenius (1592–1670), added another piece of the puzzle when he famously called for universal education and lifelong learning.

Hosting and supporting all these ideas was a culture of wealth. This does not mean that the progenitors of liberal ideas were unusually wealthy people, merely that they were supported by relatively wealthy societies. The relation between wealth and liberty rests on two basic economic principles. The first principle is that liberal laws support invention, manufacture, trade, and consequently wealth. The second principle is that the wealthy, from the shipping magnate down to the modest landowner, wish their property to be protected and consequently generate laws that safeguard individual liberties.

Writing in the late eighteenth century, Jefferson, Madison, and their colleagues had a complex but largely self-coherent humanist tradition to work with. Some of it they embodied in law, designing a government dedicated, insofar as possible, to the preservation of liberty. The rest they consigned to the safekeeping of their culture. Ideas like reason, creativity, beauty, love of nature, and respect for individual rights could not be written into law. The Founders bequeathed these ideas to an educational system that would support them and to a cultural milieu that would hold them dear.

Let us credit these men for doing the best they could at the time. But they stopped short of a key question: how to protect a republic from its own money.

As Jefferson himself was aware, the implications of liberty would be slow to evolve. It took brave leaders like Frederick Douglass, Abraham Lincoln, Susan B. Anthony, Simone de Beauvoir, Martin Luther King, Jr., and Lyndon Johnson to add the promise of human equality to law. Liberty found a rationale in the pragmatic philosophy of William James and John Dewey, a poetic voice in the verses of Walt Whitman, a policy toward nature in the environmentalism of Theodore Roosevelt and John Muir. As of today, only one major component of the pattern of liberty has conspicuously failed to reach center stage: the liberating education proposed by Jefferson.

Education for liberty is essential because liberty has two fundamental dimensions: one in laws and social works, another in the minds of men and women. Liberal education must be focused enough to give citizens an appreciation for their freedom; it must be subtle enough to make them aware of the issues inherent in free societies. Education must endow young citizens with a mental design that enables them to re-create a free society within their own minds. They must be taught to understand the benefits of liberty—and its price. They must be made aware of their place in history and their place in the community of nations. They must have some preview of the roles they will play in mature society. And not least, they must learn to tell truth from lie.

At this key task, American educators have failed—so miserably that they are still ignorant of their failure.[7]

Is American liberty, as currently enjoyed, sustainable even in America?

We may assure ourselves that American liberty is not sustainable in its present form from the emergent fact that it is not being sustained. Can we call a nation free when, for two straight terms (2000, 2004), it cannot fairly elect a president? When its human and material resources are commandeered for a colossally mistaken war? When its policies at home and abroad are arbitrated by big money? No, we are not entirely free—just free enough to mind our own business.

To appreciate this failure of liberty, we should revisit the syndrome mentioned at the outset of this chapter: the tendency of people in a democracy to devalue liberty in favor of wealth and security. We should remember that the last three two-term presidencies have all been predominantly concerned with wealth. Reaganomics (1980–88), sustained by the first Bush, was adapted by Clinton ("It's the economy, stupid!" 1992–2000) and intensified by the second Bush. We should also keep in mind that the last president who boldly advanced American liberty against moneyed interests was Theodore Roosevelt (1901–8).

The recurrent concentration on wealth by those in power has predictably advanced the prominence of moneyed interests in governance. Particularly under the administration of George W. Bush, big money increasingly influenced policy decisions in regulatory agencies, the judiciary, the arena of foreign affairs, and the national leadership itself. And the American left, instead of pressing for significant change, is buying into centrist compromise.

A case in point is the current discussion of lobbying reform. The American institution of lobbying—in which huge financial contributions are justified as free speech in action, and democracy is left to the tender mercies of quid pro quo—achieved nightmare status under the second Bush with the K Street Project. This spoils system, maintained by Tom DeLay, Jack Abramoff, and other notables, was well on its way to establishing a self-sustaining feedback loop between corporations, lobbyists, and Republican politicians before it was exposed by scandal. Yet the mainstream response to this conspiracy was uncommonly mild. As a 2006 *New York Times* headline ironically puts it, "Go Ahead, Try to Stop K Street." According to Todd S. Purdum, author of the *Times* article, as well as to liberals like Representative Barney Frank (D-MA) and Senator Dianne Feinstein (D-CA), the K Street Project was not a sign of a broken system but merely an aberration in business as usual.

If we look to liberal advocacy groups, the view does not significantly improve. In 2007, Common Cause ran a full page of quotations in favor of campaign finance reform, including this from the centrist commentator Lou Dobbs: "I've come to the conclusion that the only way we'll ever see their [special interests'] power substantially diminished, and the common good and national interest fully represented in Washington, is through the complete public financing of all elections."[8] Right on, Mr. Dobbs, but election finance reform, while desirable, is too little, too late. The tentacles of our lobbies stretch far beyond elections. Big oil, for example, spent $8.5 million to support candidates in the 2006 elections. Abramoff and company spent roughly ten times that sum on their Native American casinos operation alone. Lobbying is as constant and extensive as commerce itself. Senators, representatives, and other dignitaries are courted week in and week out. Often the more cooperative public officials, after their terms expire, are hired on by corporations at exorbitant salaries. Thus rewarded, they hurry back to the capital to work their old contacts for their new employers.

Like other K Street traditions, working *in* Washington and then *working* Washington is perfectly legal. And that's the rub. While doing and saying perfectly legal things, lobbyists are trashing the integrity of public office and degrading our political system into a government of the money, by the money, and for the money.

Can we reverse this trend? With due respect to Dobbs, I submit that the only effective means of reforming our lobbies is to bust them completely. Legally, the case against lobbies is aching to be reopened. Their chief pretext for existing is that they are a form of free speech. But if big money is a form of free speech, why aren't guns and bombs? Why, moreover, should well-padded corporations have freer speech (i.e., well-greased access to legislators) than other individuals do? And if, finally, it is not legal to lobby our police, judges, and juries, who carry out our laws, why should it be legal to lobby the people who make our laws? Lobbying in its present form is flat-out bribery, protected by a frivolous legality so self-serving that it stinks in our faces.

The task of busting the lobbies is difficult but certainly not impossible. We would not be well advised to seek help from Congress, for most of Congress is already compromised. Besides, we do not have to enact or change any laws to solve the problem. The Justice Department could take up the issue. Since it was able successfully to prosecute big tobacco for "racketeering," it will be able to devise some suitably damning charge against sycophants who loiter about our national and state capitals influencing legislation with money.

Are alternative versions of liberty available to non-Western states?

The prospects for liberty, and the mechanisms for achieving it, are most clearly apparent in the Asian "globalizing" states. Globalization is also a process of democratization. Not surprisingly, it is big money, the bugbear of Jeffersonian liberty in the United States, that is the catalyst for democracy in the industrializing countries. Nations like Thailand and the two Chinas want big business, and big business thrives best under small government. Socialism and communism lead to governments that are large and oppressive—governments that create economic stagnation. The only functioning small governments are democracies. Thomas Friedman, the widely traveled guru of globalization, quotes Sirivat Voravetvuthikun, a Thai real-estate developer who opened a sandwich shop after his business collapsed: "Communism fails, socialism fails, so now there is only capitalism. We don't want to go back to the jungle, we all want a better standard of living, so you have to make capitalism work, because you don't have a choice. We have to improve ourselves and follow the world rules. . . . Only the competitive survive."9

Mainland China, long a repressive communist regime, is democratizing its infrastructure to fuel economic growth. Although the party still wants to retain control, it cannot hold on except by encouraging economic forces of change: "China today faces a very modern paradox. . . . Political control is dependent on economic growth and economic growth requires the modernization of information technologies, which, in turn, have the potential to undermine political control."[10]

Perhaps the most dramatic case of globalization as liberalization is the Republic of China. Although the target of regular saber rattling from Beijing, Taiwan carries on a healthy trade with communist China and maintains a bustling economy of its own. A former president, Chen Shui-bian, envisioned a future Taiwan that would combine democracy, advanced technology, and environmentalism:

> As the new international order is reconstructed, the greatest mission of Taiwan's new leader is to consolidate our democratic system. . . . I believe that human beings are entitled to enjoy a beautiful natural environment as well as the convenience of advanced technology; I cannot imagine an essential conflict between the two. Therefore, the current rapid industrialization that has been accompanied by the destruction of the environment must be temporary. I believe it is time to transcend this conflict in order to achieve both environmental harmony and technological development. . . . My blueprint for the Green Valley must be extended to the entire island, based on the current successes and resources of Taiwan's silicon and computer high-tech industry. I hope that Taiwan in the next millennium will indeed become the Green Silicon Island.[11]

It is no coincidence that Chen's vision of his country as a Green Valley chimes with the love of nature that characterized Chinese culture for centuries before communism prevailed there. Democracy will not just modernize nations. It will allow them the leeway to appreciate their cultural roots.

Another reason why big money fuels democracy is that the growth of major homeland businesses transforms demographics. Nations of shopkeepers and laborers sprout engineers, managers, sales executives, lawyers, and financial experts. These well-paid professionals and their families enrich the market by demanding better services—medical care and education—so doctors and professors swell the middle class. Increased wealth opens the floodgates for markets in durable goods, appliances, entertainment, travel, and the arts. The clamor for improved information erodes barriers to free speech. A prosperous and literate citizenry emerges and begins to call for a political role in determining its destiny. The raw material of liberty has coalesced, and it grows ready to accept the imprint of ideas.

The liberal institutions that may emerge in Asia would have much in common with American democracy but would do well to learn from American mistakes. It is easy enough to see how improved commerce and increased prosperity can launch a democracy. Only wise legislation and sound education, however, can keep moneybags from dragging democracy under. Emerging democracies must learn, better than the United States has yet learned, to maintain the spirit of free enterprise while discouraging the oligarchical ambitions of big business.

But what of the United States? Has the great knowledge design of liberty, passed down to us so solemnly by the Founders, completely lost its vitality? Does that star-spangled banner yet wave o'er the land of the free and the home of the brave? At best, we wait and wonder. The administration of President Barack Obama, not yet fully staffed as I write in 2009, has already turned its attention to correcting the scandalous lapses of the previous administration in terms of corporate regulation and oversight. Similar regulatory initiatives are at work in the financial markets. America, after nearly bankrupting itself with excessive corporate liberty and self-indulgence, is at last dressing its wounds and girding for the future. But nationally, education remains a gaping crater. America, which now lags in production figures of all sorts, lags most notoriously in the production of leaders; and this deficit can be explained most succinctly by the absence of political literacy from our educational agenda. Although schools and colleges will benefit from Obama's stimuli, attitudinal change is needed even more than money. We must make the next generation literate in liberty—not only in its history but in the issues that liberty always brings to the table. There is no more urgent topic in the world today, nor any more pertinent to education.

13

Corporate Redesign and the
Business of Knowledge

Business begins with an idea. And as never before, its growth, stability, and ultimate success depend upon innovation and a continuing flow of imaginative thought. . . . The most urgent business of business is ideas.

JERRY HIRSHBERG

If you have an apple and I have an apple and we exchange apples,
then you and I will still each have one apple.
But if you have an idea and I have an idea and we exchange these ideas,
then each of us will have two ideas.

GEORGE BERNARD SHAW

Let us return to the concept, applied earlier to Jefferson and Brunetto Latini, of knowledge design. Metaphorically, the entire universe is a knowledge design, with particles and rays, in one configuration or another, telling substances how to behave and, on another scale, DNA molecules telling cells how to grow. In a roughly similar way, human agency can design systems of knowledge for a variety of purposes, including self-analysis and self-renewal. With this premise in mind, we may consider the possible effectiveness of knowledge design on those institutions most central to our economy: corporations.

In September 2000, I flew to Los Angeles to join in meetings and festivities attendant on the birth of a major high-tech start-up. By major I mean that the CEO was talking about seed money in the low billions. The angel with these billions was a corporate czar whose firm, along with so many others, was nearing the most extended reach of the economic bubble that was to burst the next year. But that fall the czar was feeling his oats. The only questions yet undecided, we fondly believed, were when he would buy in and for how much.

The buy-in never happened. Explanations of what went wrong vary, but at the root of the trouble were wretched communications between the czar and our CEO. Within months the corporation was in fragments, and the boisterous hallways of the corporate suite had fallen silent.

But it is those earlier, happier times that are of interest here. In those days, with good science and with seed money in hand and much more expected to come, we could afford to dream impossible dreams. As a consultant to the firm, I volunteered to write a corporate philosophy. It ran as follows:

1. Corporations can provide a source of new knowledge by supporting research, creating new applications, giving fair disclosure and manifesting the extent to which knowledge and meaning themselves have become central to the 21st-century economy. Conversely, they can fail to provide new knowledge by bridling research, sticking to established market channels, fixating on secrecy and ignoring the informational nature of the current economy.

2. Corporations can stabilize social wealth by accruing assets, building for the future, attracting long-term investments and paying regular salaries. Conversely, they can destabilize the

economy by asset-stripping, playing for short-term profit and showing bad faith towards their employees.

3. Corporations can renew the economy by generating, in a competitive marketplace, an endless diversity of creativity and innovation. Conversely, they can rob the economy of this renewing diversity by engaging in monopolistic and conspiratorial strategies.

4. Corporations can empower the consumer by creating products that enhance social consciousness, educate, challenge, improve communications and amplify independence. Conversely, they can disempower the consumer by creating products that promote addiction, support dependency, indulge obsessive behavior, flatter, deceive, privilege apparent gain over real value and valorize the cosmetic over the genuine.

5. Corporations can benefit social welfare by articulating a social mission, by becoming stable and responsive members of their local communities, by conversing with current social issues and by building within themselves a philanthropic dimension including mentorship, education and charity. Conversely, they can damage social welfare by ignoring these activities in an exclusive and arbitrary quest for profit.

6. Corporations can create their own cultural environments by realizing that they are at once workplace and living-space, and that their values and their mission are manifested by their architecture, time-management, professional language, communications, work ethic, festivities, outreach, leadership, promotions and new hires. Conversely, corporations who ignore these factors create a cultural desert where no one is communicative, engaged or secure.

7. Corporations can exercise leadership by guiding society to pro-

ductive new pursuits as well as by providing examples of able administration. Conversely, corporations who are ignorant of their leadership potential or who provide negative examples of leadership contribute to social stagnation.

8. Corporations can support world order by producing products that are conducive to peace, health and safety. Moreover, since all forms of empowerment are de facto potentially forms of endangerment, corporations that endow their products with control and restraint dimensions protect society. Conversely, corporations that purvey raw and unconsidered power to all comers endanger society.

My strategy in composing this philosophy was based on the contact I'd had with the CEO up to that point. He had given me to believe that his corporation would start a whole new ball game, both in terms of high profits and in terms of public welfare. I saw no reason why a corporation that would be raking in billion-dollar profits could not afford to help preserve the environment, hold itself to high ethical standards, and provide a variety of benefits to its employees and the world at large.

By the standards suggested in this book, such a company would "tell the truth" to its clients and employees, as well as to society at large.

The CEO read my corporate philosophy, and when he saw that it consistently characterized corporate activity in moral terms, he responded that it would not allow him enough freedom in running the firm. A group of high-tech entrepreneurs that I chaired at the Foresight Institute conference in Silicon Valley in 2001 endorsed a similar view. Free markets, they claimed, create their own forms of order. I replied to them that morality is implicit in all human dealings and thus is ignored at our peril.

Market Morality

The Alan Greenspan–Ayn Rand view that markets create moral order, thereby relieving executives of moral responsibility, thoroughly permeated the strategies and tactics of high-tech start-ups during the late 1990s and the early years of the current century. The companies took shape in a void of design and obeyed principles that might be called squeaky wheel, touch parking, go for it, and hit the beach running. Among the results of such irresponsible and chaotic growth were skewed communications and inconsistent leadership—results that led to widespread misunderstandings, epidemic dishonesty, and constant surprises. For corporate giants like Microsoft and Enron, market-determined morality courted far greater disasters. Soon corporations that had grown chaotically and without self-regulation were paying the piper. The market had finally imposed order on them. But it was not exactly the sort of market that they had thought it was and not exactly the order that they had hoped for.

These events raise a few questions. How can we get corporations to behave themselves? Can changes in corporate structure produce a saner and more dependable marketplace? Is it possible to design a corporation?

But before turning to these questions we must reconsider exactly what a corporation is. Aside from the dizzying variety of supplies and services that they produce, corporations at heart are all alike. Basically, a corporation is a suite of offices and a bunch of suits. What do the suits mainly do? They handle knowledge. They receive knowledge from the outside world or from each other. They interpret knowledge, discuss knowledge, produce knowledge, trade in knowledge. We may say with a kind of crude accuracy that essentially business is the knowledge business.

The theory of the centrality of knowledge in economics was put forth in 1945 by the economist Friedrich von Hayek. The implications of Hayek's theory in terms of corporate management form one aspect of the emerging field known as knowledge management. Without too much injustice to Hayek, we may extend his theory as follows: If corporations are intrinsically based on knowledge, the products of corporations—be they goods or services—are themselves modules of knowledge. These products not only represent the knowledge that went into their creation but also increase or enhance their users' knowledge of the world. Let us look at some of the ways corporations can be reconsidered in terms of the theory of the centrality of knowledge.

Knowledge Management and Communications

The phrase *Information Age* is predicated on the development of highly effective electronic means to generate, communicate, and store information. But information is not yet knowledge. To create real knowledge, information must be both understood and communicated effectively. It is only through understanding and communicating that knowledge can be employed in the creation of value.

The people who best understand and communicate knowledge realize, at least intuitively, that knowledge comes to us in two distinct forms and that each form demands its own distinct type of knowledge management. As Hayek puts it, "Today it is almost heresy to suggest that scientific knowledge is not the sum of all knowledge. But a little reflection will show that there is beyond question a body of very important but unorganized knowledge which cannot possibly be called scientific in the sense of knowledge of general rules; the knowledge of the particular circumstances of time and place.

It is with respect to this that practically every individual has some advantage over all others in that he possesses unique information of which beneficial use might be made, but of which use can be made only if the decisions depending on it are left to him or are made with his active cooperation."[1]

Hayek here is revisiting philosophical ground staked out by Parmenides and Plato in examining the issue of the One and the Many. Hayek's idea of scientific knowledge is analogous to the One: it is fixed, demonstrable, abstract. His idea of "knowledge of the particular circumstances of time and place" is analogous to the Many: elusive, personal, and subject to change. This second form of knowledge is implicit in Michael Polanyi's theory of apprenticeship: "You follow your master because you trust his manner of doing things even when you cannot analyze and account in detail for their effectiveness. By watching the master and emulating his efforts in the presence of his example, the apprentice unconsciously picks up the rules of the art, including those which are not explicitly known to the master himself. These hidden rules can be assimilated only by a person who surrenders himself to that extent uncritically to the imitation of another."[2]

How can a corporation account for both types of knowledge? By establishing a duplex infrastructure of knowledge management. Scientific knowledge will be arranged as it has always been: by communications to and from a centralized knowledge bank. Nonscientific knowledge will be nurtured by creating personal relationships via tutorial, conviviality, seminar, mentorship, and internship. Scientific knowledge will be communicated via scientific symbol and strict analysis. Nonscientific knowledge will be communicated via narrative, humor, and example.

If the real power of a corporation rests more in its channels of communication than in its hardware and software, other strategies are indicated as well:

Architectural design encouraging the free flow of ideas. Corridors with windows and built-in conversation nooks. Private offices not only connected with corridors but communicating across a courtyard.

Transparency from the top. Top management sets the tone by respecting employees' intelligence, stepping up to take responsibility, and adopting a policy of disclosure while also remaining open to communications from all.

Nonstop town meetings held via chat rooms and other interactive Web sites.

The use of retreats and mini-retreats to open up new levels of dialogue.

Campus-style facilities (library, fitness room, espresso bar, café, restaurant, etc.) to establish and sustain new networks of communication.

Communications with the outside world, coordinated by a single office.

Strategies of this sort are unlikely to evolve out of existing conditions. They work best when implemented all at once, as they might be by an incoming CEO.

What happens when these considerations are ignored—when big shots fail to recognize the centrality of knowledge—is a comedy of errors played out with red ink and closings. I have fictionalized two of my less savory consulting jobs, which nonetheless may prove illustrative:

I once traveled to an eastern US city to brief the staff of a prominent foundation that I'll call the Bunch of Money Institute. I boarded the plane in some trepidation, for I had actually received two different invitations, one official and one from underground. The official invitation, along with a promise to pay expenses, came from the foundation's director. The underground invitation, along with demands for me to observe total secrecy, came from a previous director, who had learned from a spy that I was on my way. She wanted me to brief her on what I saw and heard during my visit. And what I saw and heard was rather damning. The Bunch of Money Institute staff, who were supposed to be handling areas of knowledge critical to America's future, were cruelly housed in a little warren of stuffy, cramped, and poorly interconnected offices. Corporate disregard for healthy communications was glaringly evidenced by the lack of a single conference room. The director, who busied himself with policy statements and diplomatic junkets, treated staff members aloofly, and staff members told me that the foundation was divided into bunkers with competing secrecies.

Situations of this sort regularly develop in organizations that do not value knowledge, and when they develop, they unfailingly cripple the effort to achieve the organizational mission. Nor are such failures in communication confined to hidebound, top-down corporate structures. They inhere even in tiny start-ups, where the entire staff sit together in a single room. Here, poor communications are a function of ignorant leadership: of chief executive officers and chief operating officers who hoard information rather than enriching their colleagues with its power. Ironically, these executives are often oblivious to valid information that is available from the lower echelons or from outside sources. Instead, they remain intent on shoring up public relations, grasping for short-term benefits, and refining their mechanisms of control.

One such CEO, whom I will call Custer Drywall, founded a software start-up at the turn of the new century. Now and then he invited me over as a consultant. When I told Cuss that I had worked out a way his firm could enhance information flow and save tens of thousands of dollars every year, he did not trouble himself to ask me what my idea was; instead, he told me to speak to his secretary about it. Cuss kept his fellow executives completely in the dark about key issues and then complained that they were uninformed. His relations with investors were so bad that six months after his firm went bankrupt, many stockholders did not know that their money had disappeared.

Cuss was the equivalent of a knowledge black hole. In the first place, he lacked the communication skills necessary to convey an insight or drive home a point. Second, even if he had possessed such skills in surplus, he had not the slightest desire to communicate anything of substance to anybody. Third, even if he had had both skills and desire, he had no pertinent knowledge to communicate! Poor knowledge-handling of this sort has driven many firms, small and large, to ruin since the turn of the current century. And the failures will continue until corporate policy comes up to speed with a knowledge-driven marketplace.

Knowledge as Authority

In a knowledge-based economy, respect must be awarded to the knowledgeable, no matter what their level of seniority. This presupposes a management structure flexible enough to let a junior colleague set the agenda if he or she carries moral authority on the day's topic. This also means living by the premise that knowledge is the only dependable source of success. An excerpt from a Lotus advertisement suggests the enshrinement of knowledge in the corporate value system: "MERE MORTALS MANAGE PEOPLE AND MONEY. YOU MANAGE THE KNOWLEDGE OF THOUSANDS. When you can find the best person for the job in your global organization, that's knowledge management for e-business. When your company's best thinking is just a few clicks away, that's knowledge management for e-business. When you can bring all this together instantly, that's knowledge management for e-business. How do you do it? With super.human.software that helps e-business people work together."[3]

Knowledgeability can be promoted not only by rewards and promotions but also by bringing onto the corporate campus courses that lead to forms of certification.

A Knowledge-Intensive CEO

The CEO of a knowledge-centered firm should not only reward knowledgeability but also be the most variously knowledgeable person in the corporation. Only thorough knowledgeability will enable the CEO to prioritize corporate aims and to translate the concerns of one branch to the corporation as a whole. The responsibility to translate suggests another talent required for leadership. The CEO must be an expert at demystifying knowledge, of making the achievements or concerns of one specialist available to another. We have heard time and again that CEOs ought to be excellent communicators. Now let's make sure that each of them has something to communicate.

A Chief Knowledge Officer

The preeminence of knowledge in business suggests that a corporation would be well served by hiring on a chief knowledge officer at the rank of vice president. This CKO would be qualified in the latest methods of knowledge management, would facilitate and oversee the flow of information within the company, and would coordinate various exchanges of knowledge with the outer world, from learned conferences to advertising. The Office of Knowledge would number among its responsibilities the maintenance of the corporate library and the administration of courses and the invitation of guest lecturers. Most important, along with the CEO, the CKO would also be responsible for establishing and upholding the values of a knowledge-based corporate culture. The CKO would remind colleagues when necessary that the intrinsic worth of a corporation is dependent on the good it brings to the world at large. The CKO would keep the corporate conscience alive and well. Finally, along with the CEO, the CKO would preside over a corporate culture in which the most valuable forms of knowledge were expressed in the language of ideas.

Corporate Consciousness

A young chemical company once asked me to find out how it could approach a huge pharmaceutical corporation with a new application. I picked up the phone, appealed to a few contacts, and after a few hours finally reached a human voice in the giant firm's research division. The chat was friendly enough, but during my telephone peregrinations, the implicit message had been eloquent: the last place on earth to approach with the results of your own research is a corporate research division. Its staff cannot help but see your approach as a threat to their job security. But in this chapter we are designing a different kind of corporation: one that prioritizes knowledge so thoroughly as to create a form of group consciousness. This consciousness makes the company more effective in handling knowledge from inside and from outside; it also provides perspective on the external social issues relating to corporate strategy. Through such a perspective a corporation can reach out for the most valuable knowledge of all: a self-knowledge that can position it in the healthiest part of the market and guard it against abuses from without and within.

The strategies outlined here are intended to open up a fresh perspective on corporate design in the twenty-first century. To set up a corporation centered around knowledge is to place that corporation in a moral universe, a context in which the behavior of any economic segment affects the well-being of the whole marketplace. "Conscious" corporations are able to consider which strategies will strengthen and enrich the marketplace and which will not. Wise planning of this sort may sacrifice quick profit but is likely to lead to long-term growth. Market-determined morality, on the other hand, with its attendant opportunistic and exploitive strategies, is a sure ticket to trouble in a knowledge-based culture.

A Postscript on Google

All this should throw new light on the phenomenon that is Google .com. Google is an enormous knowledge shop, an intellectual emporium whose users enter and prosper for free. And Google does not merely dispense knowledge. It organizes, enhances, refines, decorates, demystifies, empowers, and mobilizes the knowledge that is its substance. More fully than any other engine of its sort, more aptly than the proudest universities, Google realizes the character of knowledge, not just as the source of human wealth but as the most essential form of wealth conceivable. In so doing, Google reaches a new juncture in the evolution of the marketplace. Google is special in three major areas: marketing strategy, business model, and underlying intention.

Google's Marketing Policy

Colleges and booksellers, who dominated the knowledge market before the advent of Internet search engines, treated knowledge like any other commodity: they sold it for money. Google gives away knowledge lavishly and effectively. Giving it away is a marketing strategy because giving knowledge creates new value. It creates value among users by making them wiser and more productive and by exciting and amusing them. It creates value by building a global plaza where hundreds of millions of users congregate in their moments of greatest excitement, amusement, curiosity, and need. Advertisers build their stalls and arcades around this plaza. Advertisers pay Google for time and space.

Google's Business Model

Before the rise of search engines, the knowledge market used the traditional bipolar business model: the exchange of equal value between buyer and seller. This model worked famously, although it has always carried the threat of a conflict of interest between the two parties. In contrast, the rise of the search engine introduced—and Google has all but perfected—a tripolar model, in which users, though not directly charged for goods or services, are inspired to stimulate the economy in pursuit of their own profit or pleasure. The success of this model depends on the meeting of three requirements:

That the knowledge acquired is worth the users' effort to
acquire it
That the commerce so generated is worth the advertisers'
investment
That the advertising revenues and other revenues are adequate
to guarantee the provider a profit

To the extent that Google has met these requirements, we may discuss its business model as an early step in metacapitalist economics. It is not that Google has taken the capital out of capitalism. Quite the contrary. It is that Google has invested heroically in *human* capital—in users' energy, knowledgeability, and initiative. The value of the whole marketplace spiked in consequence. Whether intentional or accidental, the emphasis on human capital as a fiscal vector shows that capitalism can be refined from an Ayn Rand cockfight into a progressive element in social evolution.

Considering Google's tripolar money machine, we may find it hard to avoid some extravagant comparisons. Google's business model in one sense resembles Felix Wankel's legendary tripolar rotary engine, which powers cars at high speeds with a minimum of moving parts. From a more anthropological perspective, Google has harnessed the key engine of a gift culture (the money-free transfer of value) for a distinctly profit-making enterprise. This feat is economically unprecedented. To appropriate the power of the gift is to approximate the power of nature, which gives great gifts like sunshine and rain. By giving, Google has transcended the world of traditional economics and become a force of nature.

Google's Underlying Intention

Respect for knowledge has long been an elementary sign of our humanity. As the marketplace has grown more and more dependent on technology, knowledge has emerged as the dominating engine of the economy. Google has not only recognized the economic emergence of knowledge but realized in it a goldmine of value, both immediate and potential. Google's stroke of genius, from which the world may well learn, is that giving value is more profitable than selling it. Google's stated goal, "to organize the world's information and make it universally accessible and useful," is based on a premise as solid as it is revolutionary.

But, though creative in its use of knowledge, Google is far from closing the knowledge loop. That fulfillment can occur only when it widens its purview to include the social context of knowledge, the human reality that dictates the use of knowledge in an evolving world. Why is this step necessary? Suffice it to say that the technical knowledge provided by Google is currently falling under the control of people who are ill prepared to use it. These people, as current events make abundantly clear, lack the humanistic savvy to make knowledge count in arenas like international affairs, macroeconomics, social justice, media strategies, and even education. Since traditional education is falling far short of producing leaders appropriate for a knowledge culture, it figures that super-affluent players like Google may have to fill the void with educational and philanthropic programs of their own. Although iTunes (Apple) and YouTube (Google) have already taken steps in this direction by showing academic lectures on screen, much remains to be done.

Google has its share of critics, whose complaints include the charge that it dispenses knowledge without humanity. To me this means that Google neither privileges one piece of information over another nor provides a context for the use of knowledge in a diverse and unstable society. It should be clear to anybody—although it is not yet clear to corporate America—that if knowledge is the new gold dust of the economic frontier, knowledge must be treated within a moral framework that regulates and channels its power. If civilized regulation is the appropriate context for other energy sources, like nuclear power and money itself, it must be the appropriate context for knowledge, too. Google and its competitors should bend their substantial resources toward addressing the proper use of knowledge in a moral world.

14

Designing Time

Each day is a little life: every waking and rising a little birth, every fresh morning a little youth, every going to rest and sleep a little death.

ARTHUR SCHOPENHAUER

How can we speak of the architecture of time? Architecture, as we all know, comprises three dimensions, while time is known as occupying only one. Time, as we understand it, does not wander or zigzag; so its architecture should be no more than a straight line. Thinking this way, however, we miss the point. In human terms, we know space and time only by what limits or forms them. I would not be aware of space at the moment were it not for the walls of the room I sit in. Analogously, time is limited and deformed by human experience—perception, understanding, emotion—in such a way as to give it shape. If we did not experience motion and stasis around us and within our selves, our time would stand still. To speak of time design is to speak of specific and deliberate reformations of time. The design of time is any art or other activity that systematically organizes and directs our experience.

Music is an architecture in time. Listening to a flute solo is like following a garden path. Listening to a symphony is more like exploring the rooms of a palace. Joseph Haydn not only designed the formal structure of the symphony but also contrived, by brilliant variations in orchestration, to create diverting structures in time. Note especially the trio in the minuet of his *Clock* Symphony (no. 101, third movement), where he delights us with a dialogue between the full orchestra and a single flute. And as with music, so with all performing arts and many other "designed" experiences. The artist who can design and direct our time can lead us in much the same way that a conductor leads an orchestra.

How can we describe the dimensions inhabited by temporal design? Let's begin with that dimension which is the equivalent of spatial depth: *duration*. The time architect walls off a given work of temporal art with a beginning and an end. Less emphatic walls of time may separate chapters or movements within the work. The architect may also contour a work's duration by variations in pace. Imagine, for example, a work of music that is part tap dance, part waltz, and part dirge. Or tune in to Haydn's *Clock* Symphony again—this time to the second movement, where he establishes a moderate clocklike tempo, then weaves faster music around it. Music of this sort reshapes and complicates our time, delighting and exercising the mind.

The second dimension of time, equivalent to spatial width, may be termed *perspective*. How much are listeners asked to keep in mind at a given moment of experience? Earlier I compared a flute solo to a garden path and a symphony to a palace. Clearly the symphony requires of its audience a broader perspective than does the solo. Broadening the perspective of a temporal work of art increases its complexity and demands more of our attention. The gripping first scene of *Hamlet* begins with one guard, lonely and fearful, standing on the palace wall. Shakespeare speedily broadens the perspective to include three characters and then shatters this perspective with the entrance of the Ghost. In the next scene the playwright brings his full company out to crowd the stage in impressive court regalia and then suddenly narrows the focus to the single figure of Hamlet. These radical shifts in perspective exercise the audience, reminding them of the crucial distinction between public and private time.

The third dimension of time, analogous to spatial height, is *energy*. What kind of emotional challenge is the artist throwing our way, and how powerful is its charge? Beethoven, a master of emotional dynamics, shocks us with the aggressive four-chord opening of his Fifth Symphony, but he can also soothe and delight us with the opening of his Sixth (the *Pastoral*). Shakespeare harrows us with a bloody murder in *Macbeth* and then immediately lightens the tone with the tipsy ramblings of the drunken porter. Conversely, he excites us with the appearance of the Ghost in *Hamlet* and then handcuffs us with the ceremonial politeness of Claudius's court. Such abrupt changes contract and expand our sense of time.

These dimensions of time are to a large extent interlimiting. An artist cannot, for example, sustain a fast pace, a broad perspective, and high energy over a long period without exhausting the audience. Shakespeare cannot put his famous Ghost in every scene of *Hamlet*. If he did, his audience would develop Ghost-fatigue. Especially in music, theater, and cinema, the best artists vary duration, pace, perspective, and energy to sustain audience attention and to provide a variety of experiences. This rule of interlimitation will come in handy later.

Athletic Contests as Social Designs in Time

Sports, which are the cousins of the performing arts, have their own classic protocols of time. I use the word *classic* because every game—football, baseball, soccer, basketball, and all the rest—creates its own microcosm of time: a compact social world of absolute and universally recognized dimensionality. To both players and spectators, these time worlds are encompassing and transforming. Some sports (basketball, football) are controlled by fictional versions of clock time, with a game clock that officials can turn on and off. Others (baseball, tennis) dispense with the clock entirely. In games of the latter type, the innings, sets, or their equivalents become clocks of sorts, succeeding each other to the inevitable end.

Baseball is a game of anxiety and finesse. A baseball player may be completely inactive for many minutes at a time. Up to eight of the eighteen players are inactive half the time, waiting in the dugout to bat or practicing swings in the on-deck circle. Only four of the eighteen work at all regularly: the pitchers and the catchers for each team, who alternately take the field. For the other fourteen, the time warp is downright existential: occasionally full of challenge, more often like a populist version of *Waiting for Godot*. Thus understood, the time architecture of baseball comes close to imitating the time architecture of our own psychic lives. Often enough we stand in the outfield of life waiting for the crack of the bat and the approaching ball and wondering whether we will be ready for the event.

If baseball imitates life, football imitates art. Unlike baseball, football is time specific. Precisely one hour of time is allowed for each football game, to be meted out scrupulously by an official on the field. If the basic unit of baseball is the pitch, the basic unit of football is the play, a choreographic procedure intricately organized by the eleven players on offense and successfully or unsuccessfully recognized and disrupted by the eleven players on defense. Each play resembles an art form, as does the sequence in which various plays are run. Television commercials excepted, the pace is steady: spectators seldom have to wait for action. During each possession, every player is involved in every play, whether or not he comes near the ball; and this involvement necessitates a harmonized engagement with teammates as well as an informed response to the actions of opponents. Insofar as is possible in a violent sport, the game of football derives its power from esthetics and dialogism.

Briefly comparing the two sports by time dimension, we find that football is faster paced and far broader in perspective. But in overall effect, this edge in two out of three categories is not completely to football's advantage. This can be explained by the rule of interlimitation. In emphasizing pace and perspective simultaneously, football overloads the attention of players and spectators alike. Even individual plays do not reveal their subtleties until details are replayed in slow motion on video. Baseball, by contrast, is dramatic in its simplicity. Each player who touches the ball comes under scrutiny in his own brief window of time. Isolated in space and time, he can convey the full energy and urgency of his action.

Two factors regarding duration, both evident in art and athletics, should be brought to mind before we move on. These are fatigue and investment. A football team that is ahead in points will run more plays on the ground late in the game because the opponents' defensive line is tired and because plays on the ground do not stop the clock. Something similar operates in drama. Shakespeare seldom introduces major new characters or ideas late in a play because his audience may be too fatigued to digest their significance. This fatigue is to some extent relieved by investment. A football head coach and his offensive coordinator will hang on to their starting quarterback, even when his capacity is diminished by age. They are invested in him as a team leader and local draw. Similarly, Shakespeare's audience will remain seated for the full length of *Hamlet,* even though they grow fatigued and know the ending. They are emotionally invested in the performance.

We might expect that fatigue and investment would work against each other in any real-time situation. But we will soon see how, in the hands of a clever practitioner, they can be applied simultaneously.

Time Design in the Arts of Persuasion

The architecture of time is based on the architecture of human psychology. When attuned accurately to human nature, time designs can achieve highly specific responses. Time designers can control other people simply by resetting their mental clocks. Time design is thus a social tool that can be employed under a variety of circumstances, to good effect or ill. The locus classicus for this manipulation of time is the ancient art of rhetoric.

Classical thinkers saw the art of rhetoric as an indispensable instrument of political power. They were also aware that public speakers derived their power from manipulating audience psychology. By the mid-fourth century BC, a detailed time design for an ideal speech had evolved. This design for what is sometimes called Isocratic oration has survived up to the present day:

1. introduction
2. exposition
3. division into parts
4. proof
5. refutation of counterarguments
6. closing plea[1]

The classical oration plotted along these lines is a template for persuasion. Its division into discrete successive segments lends an air of systematic and plausible development. Using it, a speaker can give the impression of having great knowledge of the subject at issue and can set up an illusion of utter rationality. Conversely, the speaker can unlock pent-up audience emotions—fear, envy, anger, gratitude, compassion—and turn listeners from skeptical evaluators into an unquestioning mob. Two thousand years after Isocrates, Shakespeare conveyed this awesome power in Mark Antony's "Friends, Romans, countrymen" speech over the slain Julius Caesar. This famous speech, although it does not strictly follow the Isocratic formula, says much about the role of time design in persuasion. Antony, whose hidden purpose is to incite his audience to avenge Caesar's death at the hands of Brutus and Cassius, begins his oration by saying almost the opposite of what he means:

> Friends, Romans, countrymen, lend me your ears!
> I come to bury Caesar, not to praise him.
> The evil that men do lives after them,
> The good is oft interred with their bones;
> So let it be with Caesar.

He coyly feigns inability to continue his speech—such is his love for Caesar:

> Bear with me;
> My heart is in the coffin there with Caesar,
> And I must pause till it come back to me.

Having won the citizens' sympathy, he reverses fields and bowls them over by reading Caesar's will:

> Moreover, he hath left you all his walks,
> His private arbors, and new-planted orchards,
> On this side Tiber; he hath left them you,

And to your heirs forever—common pleasures,
To walk abroad and recreate yourselves.
Here was a Caesar! When comes such another?
                    (*Julius Caesar,* III.ii)

This final touch of pathos arouses in the crowd a violent affection for Caesar and an equally violent distaste for his slayers. The Romans rush off, intent on revenge.

Antony's speech suggests that the content of any passage of persuasive art is specific to its position in the time frame. The passage need not be sincere, or true, or contextually consistent so long as it strikes the right tone for the moment. The rhetorician controls the audience by designing their time.

Not surprisingly, time design is a key element in modern marketing. The best way to sell something big to customers is to get them to spend ample time with you. Developers and casinos will invest large sums of money to bring potential customers from hundreds of miles away. Individuals thus transported are likely to feel a heightened obligation. They will be slightly disoriented and hence more suggestible. Besides, they will have invested their time, and people do not like to invest their time in vain.

A certain high-end food market makes large profits by entrapping customers like me in a time vortex. This market has two public entrances, west and east, but for a variety of reasons, planned by the corporation, almost all of us customers enter through the eastern door. We find ourselves immediately surrounded by fruits and vegetables, attractively displayed. Directly to the right and only a few feet away are the fresh meats, poultry, and fish. As we can tell from partaking of the many free snacks, this is all good stuff, and surprisingly, the prices are comparable to those at the big chain store nearby.

If we now do a 180-degree turn and head for the checkout stands, we probably make out very well, and the market takes a net loss on our transactions. But the shop is just too pleasant for us often to go straight out, and besides, there are more free snacks to come. So we head in the only other direction possible: the bulk foods aisle. As we browse the aisles of the shop's inner sanctum, among the teas and pastas and crackers and beers, we begin to get some idea of how the market makes its money: the pricing here is that of a specialty shop. Generous in its meat and vegetable pricing, the establishment makes its killing through collateral damage.

The marketing masterpiece is saved for last. Our preordained journey toward the checkout stands takes us through the wines and cheeses, both of which are devilishly overpriced. Buying both wine and cheese here can easily up our total bill by more than 30 percent. What are the alternatives? Fight rush-hour traffic again, park in another parking lot, and go through another checkout line—and get even more exhausted than we already are. By far the least of the evils is staying put and spending a little more money. Besides, as we have moved down aisle after aisle, we have been getting hungrier and hungrier.

Another sort of time vortex inheres in American auto sales. Phone a car dealer and ask about a possible bargain, and he (it is usually a he) will insist that you present yourself physically at his lot. It's not that he's so eager to make your acquaintance. Rather, he knows from statistics that he is substantially more likely to make a sale if he can take an hour or two of your time. The beginning of your visit—the mouth of the vortex—is casual and low-keyed. You tour the lot with a salesperson, comparing models and prices. You go for a test drive and then proceed into the office to cut a deal. Here, the emotional pressure mounts. Over a period that may seem interminable, the salesperson wrangles, haggles, and pleads with you as the price of the car edges down from the sticker price to the salesperson's targeted price. Both exhaustion effects and investment effects are on the seller's side. You want to get the transaction over with, and you don't want to have wasted your time.

Time design presents itself in all enterprises of persuasion, from the "free trial" offered by mail-order companies to the vinous seduction attempt after dinner at Maxim's. Time design is dramatically present in religious ceremonies, where the obligatory repetition of sacred words and solemn gestures over an extended period reinforces belief and obedience. It is of cardinal importance in American congressional lawmaking, where committee chairs, who represent the majority party, can wield enormous power just by setting the agenda. Examples like these suggest that controlling time is little short of controlling people. Small wonder that, in the marketplace of goods and ideas, where designs tell truth or lies, time designs often tell lies.

Variatio delectat: Time and the Music of Life

Given all the ways in which time design can delight, deceive, and confuse us, we might expect it to be of some use in the fashioning of a healthy life. What does it mean, first of all, to design personal time? Or, to put it differently, how does time design differ from time management? Time management is a goal-oriented strategy, and the goal is normally linked to profit. Time design, on the other hand, can apply to a regime of mental fitness. In chapter 10, I described the daily schedule that I once observed while bringing up young children, and I observed just above that good musicians and other artists vary duration, pace, perspective, and energy to sustain audience attention and to provide a variety of experiences. What these two time designs have in common is attention and variety. Each of my daily activities required my full attention, but each challenged me in a different way. There was a refreshing contrast between the rushed pace at breakfast and the meditative solitude of writing. My perspective broadened and narrowed as I moved from family to writing to teaching and then to jogging. My expense of energy rose or fell with each succeeding activity. An equally wide variety inhered in the character of my activities. Each day demanded attention to the personal, the familial, and the professional. My daily schedule included a range of intellectual levels from Shakespeare to a Labrador retriever and a range of design challenges from a seminar syllabus to a smoked turkey sandwich. Every aspect of my normal human function was exercised on a daily basis; my life had become symphonic and was the richer for being so. As Cicero put it, "Variety delights." In my case, a variety of daily jobs, fitted closely to a variety of psychological faculties, gave my days wholeness.

Sadly, I cannot turn those experiences into some recipe for happiness, some psychological cure-all. I did not consciously choose those days. To a large extent, they were laid on me by circumstance. Theories of rational choice do not prescribe that I choose to prepare two or three meals per day, five days a week, on top of professional assignments. Or that, waking from a less than average amount of sleep, I walk a dog that has a mischievous temperament and seven times my energy. What made these days *intentional* was that they spoke to elements inside of me, in ways that I did not always understand, and called forth more from me than I thought it was possible to give.

Exactly what human elements, you may ask, are satisfied and renewed by such energetic and varied activities? There are some human desires that do not appear on the modern capitalist wish list. The list begins and ends with things that can be bought and sold: power, position, leisure, food, entertainment. The needs that I refer to cannot be bought and sold, because they speak to individual initiatives, individual needs: to give, to create, to communicate, to risk. Modern institutions are not meeting these needs, and as a result, many citizens suffer moral and psychological starvation. But my intentional days satisfied my silent hungers. Such days stretched me and refreshed my interface with the world. We remember the homeowner described in chapter 2 who discovered that "Mr. Wright had not built a house for who I was—but for the person that I could become." My own house of time had been built much the same way.

15

The Design of Private Knowledge

How do we manage the private thoughts and pent-up emotions that are the inevitable legacy of our personal experiences? To some extent, we can regulate our private knowledge consciously, the way trainers control and train a dog. But our inner energies are so volatile that conscious control inevitably proves inadequate. We can also try acting out our inner feelings, but expressing them can verge on the antisocial and the chaotic. Our private knowledge is a resident spirit alive within us, inalienable and unquiet. It is inextricably linked to emotions—grief, regret, resentment, distrust, fear, frustration—that strive to redirect our energies. It speaks to us, and we respond to its messages as best we can.

Control and self-expression do not, however, exhaust our full psychological bag of tricks. Constantly, often quite unconsciously, we design and redesign our private knowledge, humanizing it and making it manageable.

Here are a few ways this happens.

Ophelia and the Psychiatrists

On the morning of Saturday, September 15, 2001, I sat in a committee room in Ashland, Oregon, with a group of about twenty psychiatrists. We were all in various stages of recovery from the events of

9/11, and they had asked me to join them in a kind of group therapy session. I had come along with some trepidation. My role at the convention—where the doctors came annually to share research and appreciate drama—was to lecture on Shakespeare, not terrorism. How could I calm others when I was myself upset? What could I possibly say about trauma to twenty traumatized psychiatrists?

The Bard himself came to my rescue. I remembered that whenever a major character in Shakespeare dies offstage, Shakespeare concocts an eloquent speech in which details of the death are described. Here, for example, is Queen Gertrude narrating the death of Hamlet's beloved Ophelia:

> There is a willow grows aslant a brook,
> That shows his hoar leaves in the glassy stream.
> There with fantastic garlands did she come
> Of crowflowers, nettles, daisies, and long purples,
> That liberal shepherds give a grosser name,
> But our cold maids do dead men's fingers call them.
> There on the pendant boughs her coronet weeds
> Clamb'ring to hang, an envious sliver broke,
> When down her weedy trophies and herself
> Fell in the weeping brook. Her clothes spread wide
> And, mermaid-like, awhile they bore her up;
> Which time she chaunted snatches of old tunes,
> As one incapable of her own distress,
> Or like a creature native and indued
> Unto that element; but long it could not be
> Till that her garments, heavy with their drink,
> Pull'd the poor wretch from her melodious lay
> To muddy death.
>
> (Hamlet, IV.vii)

Shakespeare's stage strategy is apparent here. He cannot drown Ophelia in front of the audience, so he does the next best thing: he has another character describe the death in memorable detail. But it also occurred to me that the death narrative was more than just a stage tactic. It was a cross-cultural folk tradition, affecting us all and born of a universal psychological necessity. Whenever we hear that someone important to us has died, we want to know every possible detail, and whenever we are in control of the details, we feel obliged to pass them on to someone else who cares. The death narrative offers a kind of relief. It cannot curtail our mourning, but it can bring an otherwise intolerable truth into the realm of day-to-day reality.

How did all of this relate to the psychiatrists and 9/11? That Saturday, when my turn came to speak, I spoke to them about narrative as a means of organizing reality. I put it to them that the first step in healing after a traumatic event is to construct a narrative that places the event within a rational context. A narrative allows the mind to couch the traumatic event in knowable terms; a narrative stabilizes an injured mind much the way a splint stabilizes a damaged limb. With this in mind, I suggested that they all find out as much as they could about 9/11 and construct narratives of their own.

When I returned home to Portland, I got my hands on the most widely discussed recent book on healing after a traumatic experience, Dr. Judith Herman's *Trauma and Recovery*. To my relief, Herman's clinical experience suggested that narrative held a key position in recovery: "The next step is to reconstruct the traumatic event as a recitation of fact. Out of the fragmented components of frozen imagery and sensation, patient and therapist slowly reassemble an organized, detailed, verbal account, oriented in time and historical context. The narrative includes not only the event itself but also the survivor's response to it. . . . The ultimate goal . . . is to put the story, including its imagery, into words."[1]

My experience with the psychiatrists told me about the profound importance of design in human psychology. To begin with, a narrative, no matter how accurate, is not the event that it describes; it is instead a mental design that emulates the event, embodies it in rational discourse, and allows us to tolerate and control it. Our very ability to give things shape is a kind of spiritual medicine that heals our wounds. Once we have digested a narrative, it becomes part of our mental continuum, the grand set of designs that constitutes our reality. Nor is our human tapestry of narratives limited to personal experience. We locate ourselves and our culture in the great system of narratives called history. We comprehend and manipulate our physical reality through a web of narratives called science. Only through such elaborate sets of narrative designs can we relate to the world around us, relate to each other, solve problems, and appreciate life. The trauma narrative is part of the formidable anthology of narratives, some precise, others poetic, that we construct and that construct our humanity.

Narrative and the Unconscious

Most trauma narratives are not ordered by therapists and constructed on purpose. We create them unconsciously, and unconsciously they become part of our self-healing. Whenever I think of my mother's death in 1996, I impulsively frame it in a narrative that includes her illness and diagnosis, an operation, my visits from afar to see and help her, my last goodbye. It is a sad story, but it shields me from an otherwise unbearable sense of loss. I did not create this story on purpose. My mind fitted it together unconsciously, in part as a means of navigating the wilderness of grief. In this I am no different from most other people. Like idiot savants, we are unconscious novelists and playwrights, spinning narratives that help us negotiate with our inner demons. These semi-fictions save us from crushing guilt and the quagmire of denial.

In the same sense that we are unconscious creators of trauma narratives, we derive cathartic satisfaction from the trauma narratives of others. The disaster movie, for example, is popular not only because it excites our fear and pity but also because, almost without exception, it locates disaster within a rational context and shows that life goes on. The most important part of our survivor narrative, its hidden gleam of redemption, is that we survive. The disaster narrative functions as a design for healing. My post-9/11 reading includes *102 Minutes: The Untold Story of the Fight to Survive Inside the Twin Towers,* by Jim Dwyer and Kevin Flynn. Dwyer and Flynn have winnowed a mountain of information into a narrative involving scores of survivors and victims and focusing on the monstrosity of the event and on the humanity of those whom it affected. One of the reasons I am reading this book is that it helps me reify the event and set it in a human context. I open the book, skip to the end, and read about one of the rescuers: "Just as people had come to work hours earlier, at the start of the day—an entire age ago—now Chuck Sereika was starting for home on his own. His old paramedic shirt torn, he plodded north in the late-summer night, alone, scuffling down streets blanketed by the dust that had been the World Trade Center."[2] Unthinkable events have occurred, and people have suffered unthinkably. But life goes on. A man is walking home.

My Own 9/11 Narrative

When I suggested to the Ashland psychiatrists that they create narratives of 9/11, I had no idea what tricks this disaster would play on my own mind. In short order I became politically galvanized. For the next two years I did not write anything but essays connected with civic education and civic action. In the summer of 2004, shortly after I commenced work on this book, I had a sudden opportunity to revisit 9/11 anew. I had learned by chance that Minoru Yamasaki, the architect of the World Trade Center, had not been enamored of its final design but had been coerced by the Port Authority to scrap his original plans and build something twice as big. I set out to investigate the compromises that Yamasaki had had to make and their effects in human terms. I decided to publish my findings in a chapter called "Design as Tragedy." I had already begun to write the chapter when I made an unsettling discovery. Examining a photograph of the wreckage, I found a nuance of Islamic design (Persian pointed arches) in the metal tracery that was still standing. I Googled a couple of key words and within seconds was looking at a detailed scholarly analysis of Yamasaki's deliberate use of sacred Islamic imagery in the Twin Towers and their adjacent square. I learned as well that Yamasaki had done major westernizing projects in Saudi Arabia during the 1960s and that these projects had brought him close to the Saudi royal family, as well as to the Bin Laden construction firm. This research convinced me that Yamasaki's work in Arabia, and his well-meaning adoption of Islamic imagery, were why Osama bin Ladin, a fundamentalist Islamic who detested westernization and the Saudi royals, had targeted this architectural complex, above all others, in 2001.

The chapter that I wrote then (a revised version appears in this book) was an effort at investigative reporting and an object lesson in how corporate priorities can adversely affect design. But I later realized that it was something else as well. For better or worse, it was my version of a trauma narrative, a psychological mechanism for coping with chaos.

The Design of Memory

Like narratives, memories are created designs whose origins are mainly unconscious. Consciously created memories—phone numbers, travel schedules, answers to trivia questions—are like a thin film over a vast sea of living images, ideas, emotions, and characters that, willy-nilly, populate our notion of the past. While many people treat these memories as solemn truth, experience proves that they are at best mixtures of fact and fancy, often tinged with a self-defensive bias or warped by some other subjectivity. Each party in a two-way spat, for example, is likely to remember the other party as the aggressor. More interestingly, the mind can unconsciously alter memories to make them more suitable for its own Byzantine purposes. For these and related reasons, memories can be studied as designs.

My own earliest memory is of being carried around by my maternal grandmother, who always sang me the same song, the main theme from Franz Lehár's *Merry Widow Waltz*. This memory conveyed a sense of pride. Although my three other grandparents had come from unlettered European villages, I liked to think that my grandmother had anointed me, early on, with a soupçon of nineteenth-century Viennese culture. But this fanciful structure later fell like a house of cards. Lehár, I discovered, was a twentieth-century composer who lived until the late 1940s. Worse yet, I found out that the *Merry Widow Waltz* had been available to my grandmother via Jeanette

MacDonald's blockbuster rendition in Ernst Lubitsch's 1934 movie, *Merry Widow*. Once robbed of its pleasing symbolism, my memory of being sung to began to fade.

Another case in point is a "first memory" recounted to a large audience in Istanbul by the intrepid Middle East hand Cornelius Bull. When he was a toddler in the late 1920s, he was sitting on his father's shoulders as they toured a zoo. They stopped at the elephant pen, and his father handed him a peanut with instructions to feed it to the giant animal. The child reached out across the top of the fence, and the elephant obligingly extended its long snout until it was only inches away. But this was too much for young Cornelius, who withdrew his hand in fear. Then, as though delivering a lesson, the elephant whacked him on the head with its snout.

An eloquent—perhaps too eloquent—first memory. For anyone who knew Cornelius Bull, the fit is almost too good to be true. He was a man like his name, bold and forceful. He left a teaching career to found a successful consultancy and, in addition, played a major role in bringing modern Western education to Middle Eastern states. What could have been a more appropriate first memory for him than an elephantine lesson in courage? And what better place to tell the tale than exotic Istanbul? This is not to question Bull's honesty, although good storytellers can be expected to wield a certain license. The likelihood is that over the many years of his life, this memory began to take precedence over other early memories precisely because it was so richly appropriate to his self-image.

A final example of memory as design is from the life of President Woodrow Wilson. He claimed that his earliest memory was from 1860. He remembered a man riding up to his family home and telling Wilson's father that civil war was at hand. I doubt that this was actually Wilson's earliest memory, but it was an extraordinarily convenient one, because it linked him radically to his nation's history and because he became, in 1917, the first president since Lincoln to lead his nation into a major war. Here, as with Bull, there is a strong chance that the memory was self-selected to conform with its possessor's characterological design.

This interplay between personal history and psychological necessity brings us back to the work of Judith Herman. In Freudian psychotherapy, patients are encouraged to form narratives of long-past personal events; Freud taught that such events can spawn psychological mechanisms that reach into adulthood. Herman argues that narratives serve a second purpose as well, in offering a measure of autonomy to abuse victims who otherwise might remain traumatized. But in a lively debate now known as the memory wars, some psychotherapists have questioned the extent to which a patient's reconstructions of early childhood should be encouraged. Two points seem to be at issue here. The first is that a narrative teased from a patient by a therapist might place blame for abuse on the wrong shoulders. The second is that patients often use abuse narratives as psychological crutches; in the narratives they are victims, which frees them from taking responsibility for their own actions. In this absence of consensus, we may conclude that narrative, like any other form of medication, can be misused. But the danger confirms its power.[3]

The Design of Dreams

If narratives and memories contain strong elements of design, what about dreams? First off, we must allow that every dream on record has already been redesigned twice: once when it was converted into a memory, and again when it was recounted as narrative. But what about the dream itself? Sigmund Freud's meticulously detailed interpretation of dreams is now under widespread attack by professionals in the field, but it is still fairly clear to all that dreams convey a kind of truth about the self and that dreams are emotionally expressive. As a working hypothesis, why not entertain the premise that expression of inner emotion is the purpose of dreams?

This premise works fairly well when I have a go at interpreting my own dreams or those of people near me. It also roughly accords with the Freudian tradition, though without being as ambitious or as ruthlessly specific. But there remains the question of whether dreams achieve expression because they are based on specific patterns or designs. With regard to my own dreams, I can answer this question in the affirmative. The design that characterizes these dreams may be called cyclical recurrence.

Let me share with you my own favorite dream and the only dream that I remember in all its detail. It has occupied my sleep on more than one occasion and in various versions, but always in the early fall, just before my college classes began:

> Rising from bed at my home, I observe from the clock that I must leave soon in order not to be late for my first class. I am shot through with anxiety. I grab my things and rush out to my truck. I turn the key in the ignition. The truck does a lot of whining and screeching but will not start. *Will I miss my class?* Finally the old engine roars into life, and I am off to the campus. Arriving there, I grab a course schedule and hurry across the quad to a classroom building. In its main hall I check my schedule for the room number. It turns out that the room does not exist. I am in the wrong building. *Will I miss my class?* I race across campus to the right building, enter the right classroom, and find it packed with students. I stand before them and see

that they are looking at me rather strangely. I follow their eyes downward and discover that I have forgotten to put on my pants.

This dream is a textbook example of the subject that in one form or another dominates many dreams. With apologies for the technical language, I will call this subject "wishes and anxieties relating to the social construction of self." We often dream about how we want to show ourselves to the world and about what we fear may happen when we do. The symbolically fitting topic of the dream is how well or poorly I will do in my teaching job. Note that the dream has three episodes, each marked by a crisis that must be survived: the uncooperative truck, my choice of the wrong building, and the forgotten trousers. Truck, building, and trousers are all symbols of my anxiety, while my determination to start the truck, find the right building, and appear before my class symbolize my wish to show forth adequately in society. The reason that wish and anxiety recur cyclically is that my wish to perform always triggers its own appropriate anxiety, and the anxiety in turn provokes me to reassert the wish.

This admittedly hasty visit to dreamland suggests nonetheless that dreams concern design in two important areas. Dreams are unconscious designs for expressing the life issues that concern us. And they often concern the ways that we, professionally and personally, design ourselves for the world.

Subjectivity as Unconscious Design

The necessity of navigating life compels each of us to create an inner model of the world as we perceive it, and our success or failure in life depends in large measure on the adaptive value of the model we create. Even the most accurate copies, however, remain our own creations; and to this extent we are all amateur global designers.

Shakespeare was among the first artists to exploit this subjectivity. Each of his major characters suggests a special construct (*Gestalt*) of experience. Richard III asserts that circumstance, which crippled and deformed him, has turned his world into a theater of spite:

> I have no brother, I am like no brother;
> And this word "love," which greybeards call divine,
> Be resident in men like one another,
> And not in me: I am myself alone.
>
> (Spoken as Gloucester
> in *Henry VI, Part 3*, V.6)

King Lear, on the other hand, has been flattered so preposterously at court that his inner world has taken on a completely self-indulgent shape. When his daughter Cordelia at last refuses to flatter him, the shock shatters this personal cosmos, threatening his sanity:

> O most small fault,
> How ugly didst thou in Cordelia show!
> That, like an engine, wrench'd my frame of nature
> From the fix'd place; drew from my heart all love,
> And added to the gall.
>
> (*King Lear*, I.iv)

Lear's "frame of nature" is his inner world, a subjective construct of assumptions and omissions that is scrambled into chaos when a loved one questions its premises. So it is with Shakespeare's other great tragic heroes. Richard II, Hamlet, Othello, and Macbeth all suffer from broken inner paradigms. Conversely, it is the trickster figure, capable of coping with more than one reality, or even altering the realities of other characters, who is Shakespeare's true hero. Prospero, the mind-altering magician in *The Tempest,* conveys moral teaching through artful illusion and becomes the image of his creator, a man of many minds.

After Shakespeare, subjectivity went on to become a major theme in modernism and is in fact the primary assumption of the so-called poststructuralism heralded by Jacques Derrida (1930–2004) and Michel Foucault (1926–84). A rough interpretation of their work— which admittedly is neither simple nor self-conforming—suggests that we are all imprisoned in mental constructs that simultaneously imitate the phenomena around us and wall us off from these phenomena. Poststructuralism has served inquiry by taking the doctrine of subjectivity to its most extreme formulations, but at the expense of ignoring or painting over a number of critical questions. To name three of them:

> If the stain of subjectivity is universal, why doesn't it cover postmodernism itself?
> Why do some people engage external reality so much more effectively than others?
> What makes hard science subjective?

Questions like these reveal the Achilles' heel of poststructuralism: its insistence on enshrining subjectivity in a self-indulgent construct that is as limiting as any of the constructs that postmodernism attacks. The poststructuralist movement is, in Hamlet's words, "hoist with [its] own petard."

But just because the scope of subjectivity has been exaggerated does not mean that we should discount its importance. Subjectivity can be a major obstacle to personal success and a serious threat to mental stability. A great many psychiatrists would file for welfare benefits if only we could each think our way out of our own private Idahos. Conversely, no event is as fortunate or as difficult as the enlargement or refreshment of one's personal perspective.

The trouble is, however, that subjectivity is not mere ignorance. Rather, it is a form of unconscious design. Assume for a moment that the things about which we can feel fairly certain are arranged like dots on an otherwise blank page. Subjectivity is created when the mind draws lines connecting these dots—designs to fill in the areas of its own ignorance. Sometimes we are aware of the schemata as hypotheses: premises to be modified by study or experience. But sometimes the premises prove to be such convenient coping devices that we allow them to harden into confirmed opinion. Self-serving fictions are much less intrusive than nonconforming facts. And we tend to defend our fictions when they are challenged. Our castles of ignorance are so fiercely guarded that the creativity consultant Roger von Oech was inspired to title his books *A Kick in the Seat of the Pants* and *A Whack on the Side of the Head*.

All this aside, we may conclude that while subjectivity is natural and inevitable, it does not justify radical skepticism. Subjectivity is simply one of our means of mapping the world around us with our personal designs. The value of our designs depends not only on their comparative accuracy but on our willingness to test them in the field through dialogue and engagement. They constitute our handmade intellectual furniture, which rises in worth as we optimize our mental window space.

Design as a Quest for Order and Connection

The psychological wellsprings of conscious and purposeful design can be seen in a child's efforts to perceive and construct order from the welter of passing experience. I began to keep a journal at age thirteen, but since age six I had been packaging time in a less orthodox way. Probably thanks to my mother, I had access to a large scrapbook with red cardboard covers. Every June I would construct a graphic page in this scrapbook, each with its own unique design, to commemorate my experiences over the past academic year. That scrapbook is long lost and now little more itself than a scrap of memory. I have no clear memory, either, of what impelled me, at such an early age, to start making it. My only clue is the Jerome Kern–Ira Gershwin song, "Long Ago and Far Away," which began playing on radios around my sixth birthday. It became my favorite childhood song and evoked in me an almost pathologically premature nostalgia—a sentimentality so overwhelming that, remembering the song today, I can experience it. Probably this nostalgia provided the impulse to preserve passing time, so that it might not be totally lost, by designing it into the pages of my scrapbook. Earlier I referred to the act of design as self-empowerment and self-renewal. My own childhood experience suggests that design may also be seen as a survival skill, a self-protective means of coping with change and loss.

This exploration of designs in narrative, memory, dreams, and even apparent realities may be dismaying. But the mind's preference for its own conveniences over what we may call the inconvenient truth suggests an inborn creativity: an ability to participate seriously in design that is latent in each of us, to be perfected by schooling and liberated by will. We all have designers imprisoned within us, and the only question is whether we are able to free them.

Epilogue:
Designing Truth

Nearing our destination, we turn back for one last look at the ground that we have covered. We look down a canyon of contrasts. To one side are arrayed the instances of poor design that we have visited: the top-heavy refrigerator waiting to pounce on its owner, the ungainly Edsel whining for gulps of gas, the "Regulus" software deliberately conceived in a vacuum, the pedantic *Landschaft* of the would-be dictator, his hulking and monstrous Hall of the People, the haughtily institutional facade of Maderno's St. Peter's Basilica, and the intimidating towers of the World Trade Center—all linked to the quest for power and money, all complicit in a culture of lies. To the other side we contemplate a less massive but much more graceful medley: the elegantly tricked-out Norton motorcycle, the accommodating furniture of Charles Eames and Bill Stumpf, the surprisingly personal software of Google and Corel, Bramante's original conception for St. Peter's, the architecture of delight at the Palazzo Te, the Montefeltro Palace expressing the soul of a single individual, Sofonisba's self-portrait as a tribute to the wit and power of art. True, these examples of good design owe their own debt to money and power—as do we all. But money and power are neither their message nor their goal. They speak to us directly of life. And as they speak, they teach the truth about us and our world.

With such teaching in mind, we proceeded to visualize designs that have no specific material models: designs for living. Sen no Rikyu redesigned the tea ceremony as a means of replacing the unbalanced and ineffective interactions of his society with a cultural dialogue that was simple, egalitarian, and humane. When Baldassare Castiglione conceived of *The Book of the Courtier,* he envisioned a new society, anchored in sound knowledge and committed to individual achievement and social reform. Thomas Jefferson framed the Declaration of Independence and the Statute of Virginia for Religious Freedom as a means of building a society based on reason, self-determination, and individual conscience. Rikyu, Castiglione, and Jefferson designed more than rules and prescriptions. They designed the knowledge that made us free.

It is no coincidence that both Castiglione and Jefferson wrote under the influence of Marcus Tullius Cicero. Castiglione patterned his writing style on Cicero's, and he repeatedly quoted his words and ideas. Jefferson and his colleagues based their notion of a free state on Cicero's assertion of natural law. Jefferson composed his declaration and his statute in Ciceronian terms and called Cicero the first master of the world. We must admit that this estimate had a solid basis. More than any other figure in Western history, Cicero spoke to the idea of a discourse-centered and self-determining society. Such a society would have to be free from domination by either a foreign power or a local despot. For this reason Cicero asserted and defended the liberty of the Roman republic.

Cicero's commitment to liberty made him, many years after his death, the godfather of the modern notion of liberty as it developed in thirteenth- and fourteenth-century Florence. This makes him the source of our grandest design of all: the multifaceted concept of liberty, whose gradual development we traced in chapter 12. Understanding liberty as a design is important here for two reasons. First, it allows us to realize that other societies, lacking the conceptual infrastructure that supports our own notion of liberty, will have different views of liberty and its importance. Second, it enables us to locate the excesses and deficiencies in our own system.

As we have seen, the framework of liberty cannot hold together in a knowledge-poor and environmentally depleted society; nor can it function under a government that is dominated by corporations. Because the preservation of liberty depends on a strong system of education and an environmentally sustainable economy, and because these are currently the weak links in our democracy, they deserve emergency attention. Because neither liberty nor democracy can sustain corporations that are above the law and responsible to no one, we must put an end to corporate hegemony. Liberty as we know it is always subject to attacks of poor taste and poor judgment. But we can correct our errors as long as we do not remain the victims of our own poor designs.

With all this in mind, we might do well to recast our image of freedom, from a luxury or birthright to the necessary condition for creative work. The idea of liberty itself—beloved by many, exploited by many others—would be absurd, were it not for the liberty to design.

Notes

Chapter 1. Sen no Rikyu and the Paradox of Innovation

Epigraph: Herbert Simon, "The Science of Design: Creating the Artificial," in Simon, *The Sciences of the Artificial* (Cambridge: MIT Press, 1969). This statement by Simon has been repeated many times, notably by Victor Margolin in *Design Discourse* (Chicago: University of Chicago Press, 1989), 3. Margolin has returned to this idea more recently in *The Politics of the Artificial* (Chicago: University of Chicago Press, 2002), 107, as part of his project to broaden and integrate the historical and theoretical study of design.

1. For the ladle story, see Oliver Statler, *Japanese Inn* (Honolulu: University of Hawaii Press, 1961), 32 f. More generally, see Herbert Plutschow, *Rediscovering Rikyu and the Beginnings of the Japanese Tea Ceremony* (Folkestone, UK: Global Oriental, 2003).

2. Plutschow, in *Rediscovering Rikyu,* informs us that Rikyu's "tragic death . . . made him the unquestioned tutelary deity of tea" (16).

Chapter 2. Good Design Tells the Truth

1. Ettore Sottsass, quoted in Bettijane Levine, "The Master of Delight," *Los Angeles Times,* March 16, 2006.

2. Furniture advertisement, widely quoted.

3. The year 1960 was virtually the dawn of crash testing. Mercedes-Benz crash-tested at least one car in 1959 and claims to have been the first manufacturer to do so.

4. By 2007 the Edsel had achieved mythic status in the design vocabulary. It "has

come to symbolize design failures of epic proportions, not only in the auto industry, but in other areas of life in general. Notable duds are often referred to as the Edsel-of-Something-Or-Other." Jerry Garrett, "Wheels," *New York Times,* December 28, 2007.

5. Louis Sullivan, "Tall Office Building Artistically Considered," *Lippincott's Magazine,* March 1896.

6. "Bramante wished to pile the Pantheon upon the Constantinian basilica, so that a mighty dome would rise upon a building in the form of a Greek cross. In the spring of the year 1506 Julius, in the presence of thirty-five cardinals, laid the foundations of this imposing structure, which posterity has spoiled and changed for the worse in an inexcusable manner. . . .

   "The longer they built the more they spoiled the original magnificent plans, so that the effect of the exterior as a whole is unsatisfactory. The principal mistake lies naturally in the fact that the unsuitable extension of the nave conceals the dome from one observing the basilica from a near point of view." Paul Maria Baumgarten, "Basilica of St. Peter," in *The Catholic Encyclopedia* (New York: Robert Appleton Co., 1912), available at the New Advent Web site, http://www .newadvent.org. The author of this article, though critical of the design of the basilica, speaks with great pride of its size.

7. Albert Speer, *Inside the Third Reich,* trans. Richard and Clara Winston (New York: Simon and Schuster, 1970; rpt. 1997), 74, 133–55. Also see Dietmar Schirmer, "State, Volk, and Monumental Architecture in Nazi-Era Berlin," in Andreas W. Daum and Christof Mauch, eds., *Berlin, Washington, 1800–2000: Capital Cities, Cultural Representation, and National Identities* (Cambridge: Cambridge University Press, 2005), 127–54.

8. Eames's reference to the "well used first baseman's mitt" deserves some explanation. Readers who have played hardball, or watched it played, remember the first baseman's glove as a slender, slightly elongated object that folds on itself and lies flat as a flounder when thrown to the ground. But first basemen of the 1920s and 1930s (the days of Eames's youth) opted for a more thickly padded mitt. Were Eames writing today, he would have had to use the catcher's mitt as his metaphor.

9. See, for example, Fred Camper on Pei in his review of the redesigned Morgan Library in New York: "But at least since 1978, when I. M. Pei's East Wing of the National Gallery opened in Washington, art museum additions have tended to devote half or more of their new space to grand lobbies, cafes, gift shops and

the like. Such spaces call attention not to the art, but to the museum itself and to 'fun' activities such as jewelry shopping or cappuccino-sipping. . . .

"But why—except for the self-aggrandizement of the institution—must museum architecture be something the visitor has to fight?" Fred Camper, "Too Grand for Their Art," *Newsday,* July 30, 2006.

10. Stephen Colbert pilloried Christo's *Gates* hilariously on *The Daily Show* in 2005. His segment can currently be found on http://www.youtube.com.

11. Robin Pogrebin and Katie Zezima, "M.I.T. Sues Frank Gehry, Citing Flaws in Center He Designed," *New York Times,* November 7, 2007.

12. John Galsworthy, "Quality," in Galsworthy, *Quality and Other Stories* (New York: Scribner's, 1927).

13. Raymond Chandler, *The Long Goodbye* (Boston: Houghton Mifflin, 1959).

14. "When all detailed aspects are well integrated, the best kitchen knives become an extension of the senses, with a satisfying sense of rightness, fitting into the hand almost inevitably and giving a fine degree of balance and control." John Heskett, *Toothpicks and Logos* (Oxford: Oxford University Press, 2002), 40.

15. Private source.

16. See Michael Pollan, *In Defense of Food* (New York: Penguin, 2008), 149 f.

Chapter 3. What Design and Truth Say about Each Other

1. Christopher Alexander, Sara Ishikawa, and Murray Silverstein, *A Pattern Language: Towns, Buildings, Construction* (New York: Oxford University Press, 1977).

2. Paul Graham, "Cities and Ambition," May 2008, http://www.paulgraham.com/cities.html.

Chapter 4. Design as Tragedy

Epigraph: Ole Bouman, *Archis,* no. 1 (2002).

1. Edward Tenner, *Why Things Bite Back: Technology and the Revenge of Unintended Consequences* (New York: Knopf, 1996), 5 f.

2. Roger Cohen, "Casting Giant Shadows: The Politics of Building the World Trade Center," in *Portfolio: A Quarterly Review of Trade and Transportation,* Winter 1990–91.

3. Paul Heyer, *Architects on Architecture: New Directions in America* (New York: Walker, 1978), 194.

4. "Guy Tozzoli (1922–)," People and Events, *The Center of the World: New York, a Documentary Film*, at the PBS, *American Experience* Web site, http://www .pbs.org/wgbh/amex/newyork/peopleevents/p_tozzoli.html.

5. This episode is recorded by Richard Bender in *Kajima Research Newsletter*, no. 21. "Robertson and his partner, John Skilling, were jointly responsible for the structural design of the Twin Towers. Robertson joined the Seattle firm of Worthington-Skilling in 1958. The firm worked previously with Yamasaki on a building for IBM that used an exterior structural wall of closely spaced steel pipes, giving it a strongly vertical appearance. In 1963, Worthington-Skilling competed with seven other structural engineering firms to design the World Trade Center. Skilling made the presentation, suggesting a tube structure for the exterior wall. 'Yamasaki liked the idea,' Robertson recounted, 'because it reminded him of the structure of bamboo. The Port Authority liked it because it gave them large, unobstructed floor-plates.'

   "In any fire, it is logical to assume that the weakest link in the structure will be the first to fail. The World Trade Center's floors were the weak link. Gene Corley [leader of FEMA's investigating team] said that the floor beams or trusses heated up faster than the columns because they were made of thinner steel. The floors were supported by 60-foot right angles of steel that were bolted, not welded, to the inner and outer columns. Eduardo Kausel and Jerome Connor of the Faculty of Structural Engineering at MIT also noted the lightweight construction of the entire floor system, which they described as 'flimsy.' For them, the weakest link was the way the floor system connected to the vertical members. They and others also pointed out that these connections were protected with a mineral-fiber spray, most of which was likely to have been knocked off on impact. This happened to nearby buildings when they were hit by debris falling from the Twin Towers. It suggests that there was a lot of unprotected steel after the planes hit." The Kajima Research Letter © 2002 Urban Construction Laboratory, Richard Bender, Director; John Parman, Editor. The author wishes to thank Messrs. Bender and Parman for permission to quote.

6. "But then it transpires that Mr. Yamasaki is a good acquaintance of the Bin Laden family, a fabulously wealthy dynasty of developers and builders. They have worked with Yamasaki repeatedly since the 1950s on accursed modern projects on the Arabian peninsula, thus surrendering the holy land of the Prophet to the worldly ambitions of the Saudi royal family, who have been content with vague suggestions of the Islamic visual tradition. Examples are

the King Fahd Dhahran Air Terminal in Dhahran, which is even depicted on a Saudi banknote, and the King Fahd Royal Reception Pavilion at Jeddah Airport.

"And, as though the ironic nerve had not yet been sufficiently gratified, Yamasaki went to town with his use of Islamic design elements in the World Trade Center itself: the dense filigree of the facade, the elegant pointed arches in the base and even the plaza surrounded by the maze of streets of the New York financial district which—according to Yamasaki—recalls the courtyard surrounding the Kaaba at Mecca." Bouman, *Archis,* no. 1.

7. Laurie Kerr, "The Mosque to Commerce: Bin Laden's Special Complaint with the World Trade Center," *Slate,* December 28, 2001, http://www.slate.com/id/2060207/.

8. Heyer, *Architects on Architecture,* 195.

9. For a longer look at Yamasaki's read on the World Trade Center, see his autobiography, *A Life in Architecture* (New York: Weatherhill, 1979), 112–28. His book, in which he simultaneously presents a narrative of the project's development and defends it from early criticisms, makes no mention of any issues between him and the Port Authority. Neither does Yamasaki refer to his Islamic iconography, much less explain his esthetic rationale for it, although he does characterize his design as an "oasis" and a "mecca" (114f).

10. Cohen, "Casting Giant Shadows." Eric Darton, author of *Divided We Stand: A Biography of New York City's World Trade Center* (New York: Basic Books, 2001), is even more damning: "At bottom the story of the building of the WTC is a tale of how New York's power-brokers hijacked a public agency, the Port Authority, to build a massive real estate speculation. Their goal was to use the trade center as leverage to expand Lower Manhattan's financial district—in which they were heavily invested—while driving up property values throughout the whole area. It is hard to imagine a more blatant instance of entrenched power and wealth circumventing—and in fact, subverting—the democratic process. So the WTC can also be looked at as a monument to the abuse of public trust." Darton, "New York's World Trade Center: A Living Archive," http://ericdarton.net.

11. *Asia Times,* February 13, 2003; Ada Louise Huxtable, *New York Times,* April 5, 1973. Hughes wrote in a review of a book by Filler: "Not the least odd thing about this entire episode is that it marked the only time in its twenty-five-year history when the World Trade Center got reverential reviews. At the time it

was built, you never heard a good word for it, from architects or anyone else. In general New Yorkers decried it as an out-of-scale, monotonous monster, a giant exercise in featherbedding imposed on Lower Manhattan by the then governor of New York, Nelson Rockefeller, who filled it with floor after floor of government offices. Nobody loved the thing until two planes hijacked by Arab fanatics made it compulsory for Americans to do so.

"'There was no need, nor would there likely ever be,' Filler writes, 'for ten million square feet of rentable space to replace what was lost there, any more than there had been to build the World Trade Center four decades earlier.'" Robert Hughes, "Master Builders," review of *Makers of Modern Architecture*, by Martin Filler, *New York Review of Books*, September 27, 2007.

Chapter 5. Edsel's Law

Epigraphs: Donald Norman, *The Design of Everyday Things* (New York: Basic Books, 2002); Paul Graham, *Hackers and Painters* (Sebastopol, CA: O'Reilly, 2004).

1. See Belton Y. Cooper, *Death Traps: The Survival of an American Armored Division in World War II* (New York: Random House, 1998), chap. 2. Details of Belton's firsthand commentary have been questioned, but his position remains in accord with loss records and other accounts. The inadequacy of the M4 became national news: "One tank platoon commander, quoted by the *New York Times*'s Hanson Baldwin, declared: 'Whoever was responsible for supplying the Army with tanks is guilty of supplying material inferior to its enemy counterpart for at least two years or more.' Associated Press's Wes Gallagher, in London, reported the angry reactions of men and officers 'fed up with the statements coming out of Washington praising American equipment.' A.P.'s Robert Eunson, with the Ninth Army, ironically summed up: 'Our greatest asset, of course, is manpower.'" *Time*, April 2, 1945.

2. Both the octagon and the cube held Masonic significance. The cube occurs in the design of Masonic alters. It descended to the Masons from the ancient Egyptians (where it symbolized the earth itself), via Plato's *Timaeus*, the Hermetic philosophers, and the Rosicrucians. The cube also figures importantly as a Hebrew and Islamic symbol and hence was influential on Yamasaki's design of the Twin Towers (see chapter 3 above). In planning for Poplar Forest, Jefferson may have had in mind the famous Single and Double Cube rooms at Wilton House, Wiltshire, built along Hermetic and Rosicrucian lines in the 1630s.

3. On the Monticello staircases, see Jack McLaughlin, *Jefferson and Monticello: The Biography of a Builder* (New York: Holt, 1990), 5–7.

4. An equally notable example of the same strategy in action was Sony's development of the Walkman, which was hampered by corporate secrecy policies: "Because the engineers and the software developers apparently were never introduced, getting the music into the player was laughably cumbersome. Sony approached proprietary digital-rights management as if it were guarding nuclear secrets; Apple built a security-lite system that could download music from the Internet to a computer to an iPod so simply that your grandmother could get the hang of it while brewing tea." Mark Singer, "Stringer's Way: Can Sony's British C.E.O. Save an Ailing Brand?" *New Yorker,* June 5, 2006.

5. George Stalk, Jr., David K. Pecaut, and Benjamin Burnett, "Breaking Compromises," in Carl W. Stern and Michael S. Deimler, eds., *The Boston Consulting Group on Strategy* (Hoboken, NJ: Wiley, 2006), 179.

6. The exception here is Google's collaboration with the government of the People's Republic of China in limiting access to the Internet.

Chapter 6. Designs of Darkness

1. Detailed criticism of Heidegger's pro-Nazi activities began in 1989 with Victor Farias's *Heidegger and Nazism* (Philadelphia: Temple University Press). Farias's book triggered a debate that has continued to the present.

2. Johannes Fritsche, *Historical Destiny and National Socialism in Heidegger's "Being and Time,"* ed. Joseph Margolies and Tom Rockmore; French materials trans. Paul Burrell with Dominic Di Bernardi; German materials trans. Gabriel R. Ricci (Berkeley: University of California Press, 1999), 67.

3. Here I am using the translations by John Macquarrie and Edward Robinson in Martin Heidegger, *Being and Time* (New York: Harper and Row, 1962; rpt. 1998), 434–39.

4. Emmanuel Faye, *Heidegger: The Introduction of Nazism into Philosophy in Light of the Unpublished Seminars of 1933–1935,* trans. Michael B. Smith, foreword by Tom Rockmore (New Haven: Yale University Press, 2009).

5. See chapter 3 for a list of the qualities of good product design.

Chapter 7. Face to Face with Design

1. Giorgio Vasari, "Life of Buffalmacco," in Vasari, *Lives of the Artists,* trans. George Bull (New York: Penguin, 1988).
2. "Have General Motors' stylists run out of fresh ideas, or do the old ones just seem more fun? Personally, I'm hoping they will work their way up to the befinned 1957 Bel Air, my favorite. The temptation is to say that stylewise, it's all been downhill for Chevy since then." Jerry Garrett, "2006 Chevrolet HHR: Let's Do the Time Warp Again," *New York Times,* November 13, 2005.
3. Hirshberg was hired away from GM to found Nissan Design. He describes some of his experiences with Nissan in his book, *The Creative Priority* (New York: HarperCollins, 1999).
4. Julius Carlson received US Patent #1,738,638 on December 10, 1929.

Chapter 8. Giorgio Vasari and the Permutations of Design

1. Giorgio Vasari, "Life of Leonardo," in Vasari, *Lives of the Artists,* trans. George Bull (New York: Penguin, 1988). *Lives (Le vite de' più eccellenti architetti, pittori, et scultori italiani, da Cimabue insinoa' tempi nostri,* 1550, 1568) has been variously translated and abridged.
2. On the foundation of Vasari's academy, see Carl Goldstein, "Vasari and the Florentine Accademia del Disegno," *Zeitschrift für Kunstgeschichte* 38 (1975), 145–52; and Fredrika Jacobs, "(Dis)assembling: Marsyas, Michelangelo, and the Accademia del Disegno," *Art Bulletin* 84 (September 2002), 422–48.

Chapter 9. The Lady in the Picture

Epigraph: Simon Schama, *The Power of Art* (New York: Ecco, 2006).
1. Vespasiano, *Renaissance Princes, Popes and Prelates,* trans. William George and Emily Waters; ed. Myron Gilmore (New York: Harper and Row, 1963), 104 f.
2. Giorgio Vasari, "Life of Giulio Romano," in Vasari, *Lives of the Artists,* trans. George Bull (New York: Penguin, 1988).
3. Ibid.
4. The exterior of the castello in its present form is brick that was originally faced with marble. As for the interior, "The lower part was a base or podium about 84 metres square and 10 high, consisting of a travertine wall, faced originally with

marble. Over the entrance was the dedicatory inscription, the other sepulchral inscriptions being disposed on each side of the door. Behind the travertine wall is an inner wall of brickwork 2 feet thick, into which are bonded the radiating brick walls of the vaulted chambers that surrounded the main circular drum." Samuel Ball Platner (as completed and revised by Thomas Ashby), *A Topographical Dictionary of Ancient Rome* (London: Oxford University Press, 1929), 336–38, available at William P. Thayer, LacusCurtius Educational Resource: A Selection of Articles from a 1929 Topography of Ancient Rome, s.v. "Mausoleum Hadriani," http://penelope.uchicago.edu/Thayer/E/Gazetteer/Places/Europe/Italy/Lazio/Roma/Rome/_Texts/PLATOP*/Mausoleum_Hadriani.html. In-text citations are omitted.

5. The observation was made in Ilya Sandra Perlingieri, *Sofonisba Anguissola* (New York: Rizzoli, 1992).

6. E. H. Gombrich, *New Light on Old Masters* (Chicago: University of Chicago Press, 1986), 166 f.

7. Baldassare Castiglione, *The Book of the Courtier,* trans. Charles Singleton (New York: Anchor, 1959), 357.

8. On these aspects of literary design, see Robert Grudin, "Renaissance Laughter: The Jests in Castiglione's *Il Cortegiano,*" *Neophilologus* (Spring 1974), 199–204; Grudin, "Sequence and Counter-Sequence in *Il Principe,*" *Machiavelli Studies,* 3 (1990), 29–42; and Grudin, *Mighty Opposites* (Berkeley: University of California Press, 1979).

9. Academies of this sort had sprung up all over Italy by the late sixteenth century. They were well-funded informal societies of aristocratic men who would meet to discuss artistic and learned topics. These societies supplemented courts and universities in achieving the cultural revolution of the Italian Renaissance. Vasari's Accademia del Disegno represented the first attempt to give institutional structure and permanence to an academy.

Chapter 10. In Jefferson's Footsteps

Epigraph: Allyn Freeman and Bob Golden, *Why Didn't I Think of That?* (New York: Wiley, 1997), 99.

1. Thomas Jefferson, letter to Francis Hopkinson, 1789.

2. For an in-depth view of this professional phenomenon, see Richard Florida, *The Rise of the Creative Class* (New York: Basic Books, 2002).

Chapter 11. Jefferson's Gravestone

1. "What most fascinated him and commanded his fullest attention were new projects that demanded mechanical or artisanal skill of his laborers and that allowed him to design and superintend the entire operation." Joseph Ellis, *American Sphinx* (New York: Random House, 1996), 168.

2. Compare Jefferson's copia with this famous, and copious, passage from Cicero's First Oration against Catiline:

   When, O Catiline, do you mean to cease abusing our patience?
   How long is that madness of yours still to mock us?
   When is there to be an end of that unbridled audacity of yours, swaggering about as it does now?
   Do not the nightly guards placed on the Palatine Hill—
   do not the watches posted throughout the city—
   does not the alarm of the people, and the union of all good men—
   does not the precaution taken of assembling the senate in this most defensible place—
   do not the looks and countenances of this venerable body here present, have any effect upon you?
   Do you not feel that your plans are detected?
   Do you not see that your conspiracy is already arrested and rendered powerless by the knowledge which everyone here possesses of it?
   What was there that you did last night, what the night before—
   where is it that you were—
   who was there that you summoned to meet you—
   what design was there which was adopted by you, with which you think that any one of us is unacquainted?

   (Lewis Copeland, Lawrence W. Lamm, and Stephen J. McKenna, eds., *The World's Great Speeches,* 4th enlarged ed. [Mineola, NY: Dover, 1999])

3. I discuss the copia at greater length in Robert Grudin, *On Dialogue* (Boston: Houghton Mifflin, 1996), chap. 3.

4. For some of Jefferson's strong views on education, see Robert Grudin, *American Vulgar* (Emeryville: Shoemaker and Hoard, 2006), p. 97 and note 61. How copious strategies can inform the work of architects and other designers is made clear in the thought of the great landscape designer Frederick Law Olmsted (1822–

1903): "In works of art which the experience of the world has stamped of a high grade of value, there is found a strong single purpose, with a variety of subordinate purposes so worked out and working together that the main purpose is the better served because of the diversity of these subordinate purposes. The first secures the quality of unity and harmony; the others, that of a controlled variety." Frederick Law Olmsted, *Mount Royal* (New York: Putman, 1881), part XIV.

5. Langdon Morris, *Permanent Innovation* (Lulu.com, 2006), 226.

6. Todd Johnston, letter to Robert Grudin, January 8, 2007.

7. See James's essay of the same name, first delivered as a speech during Teddy Roosevelt's second term in 1906. Harvey Mansfield, "The Manliness of Theodore Roosevelt," *New Criterion*, 23 (2005).

8. Augustus, *The Deeds of the Divine Augustus* [*Res gestae*], trans. Thomas Bushnell (copyright 1998, Thomas Bushnell, BSG), http://classics.mit.edu/Augustus/deeds.html.

9. Ibid.

10. Vitruvius, *The Ten Books on Architecture* (1914; rpt. New York: Dover, 1960), 3.

11. Augustus, *Deeds of the Divine Augustus*.

12. Regarding Freemasonry and its ties with the Templars, see Paul Naudon, *The Secret History of Freemasonry*, trans. Jon Graham (Rochester, VT: Inner Traditions, 2005), especially chaps. 1–7.

13. On Vasari's pivotal role in elevating the reputation of the artist, see *The Renaissance Imagination: Essays and Lectures by D. J. Gordon*, ed. Stephen Orgel (Berkeley: University of California Press, 1975), 24–26.

14. "About Parsons: History," at the Parsons The New School for Design Web site, http://www.parsons.edu/about/history.aspx.

15. "Blake: Artisan," at the Virtual U, Union College, NY, Web site, http://www.vu.union.edu/~blake/artisan.html.

16. Clifton Fadiman, ed., *Little, Brown Book of Anecdotes* (Boston: Little, Brown, 1985), 66.

Chapter 12. Liberty as a Knowledge Design

Epigraphs: Thomas Jefferson, letter to George Logan, 1816; Jefferson, letter to Mann Page, 1795.

1. Gaston Wiet, *Baghdad: Metropolis of the Abbasid Caliphate* (Norman: University of Oklahoma Press, 1971), chap. 5.

2. Abu Yousuf Yaqub ibn Ishaq al-Kindi, *On First Philosophy,* II.4, ed. and trans. A. Ivry, PDF format of *Al-Kindi's Metaphysics: A Translation of Ya'qūb ibn Ishāq al-Kindī's Treatise "On First Philosophy,"* with introduction and commentary by Alfred L. Ivry (Albany: State University of New York, 1974), http://www.muslimphilosophy.com/kindi/index.html.

3. On the conflict between philosophical thought and religious belief under the Abassid caliphate, see Ira M. Lapidus, *A History of Islamic Societies,* 2nd ed. (Cambridge: Cambridge University Press, 2002), 77–80. On religious resistance to the caliphate and the resultant decline of secular authority, see chapters 6–8. According to Lapidus, "The Caliphal [i.e., secular] version of Islamic civilization was inherently flawed. While Caliphs were considered the heirs of the Prophet's religious authority as well as his political leadership, they did not inherit Muhammad's prophethood" (81). Lapidus shows that religious sentiments at the heart of Islamic culture ultimately militated against free thought and secular politics.

4. Dante gives Aristotle and Averroes strikingly honorable roles in the *Inferno,* canto 4. "Sitting amid a congenial philosophers' band, Which I observed when I raised my line of vision, *Was the master of those who understand* [Aristotle]. All look up to him, all show him admiration; Here I saw Plato and Socrates, Who stand closest to him in station, Democritus, for whom chance orchestrates The world; Empedocles, Zeno and Heraclitus; Anaxagoras, Diogenes and Thales, for whom water creates Everything; I also saw Tully and Linus; Dioscorides the herb gatherer; Seneca the moralist, and Orpheus; I saw Euclid the geometer, Hippocrates, Avicenna, Galen, and Ptolemy, And Averrhoes, who commented on the great *philosopher* [Aristotle]." *The Inferno of Dante Alighieri,* trans. Seth Zimmerman (Bloomington, IN: iUniverse, 2003), 26. For Dante's sympathetic evocation of Brunetto, see canto 15.

5. Libertas became thematic in Florentine public policy as early as 1312, when the city sought to preserve its independence from Henry VII, emperor of the Holy Roman Empire.

6. In antiquity the idea of human equality was introduced by the rhetorician Alcidamas and later entertained by the Stoics, whence it descended to Cicero (*On the Laws*). Although the full implications of the idea were never realized, in ancient times it formed in part the basis for Spartacus's rebellion (Third Servile War, 73–71 BC).

7. On this issue, see Robert Grudin, *American Vulgar* (Emeryville: Shoemaker and Hoard, 2006), chap. 5.

8. Lou Dobbs, speaking on the CNN program *Lou Dobbs Tonight,* November 1, 2006, quoted in Money in Politics, "Public Financing Gains Editorial Support," Common Cause Web site, http://www.commoncause.org/site/ pp.asp?c=dkLNK1MQIwG&b=4773897. See also Dobbs, *War on the Middle Class: How the Government, Big Business, and Special Interest Groups Are Waging War on the American Dream and How to Fight Back* (New York: Viking, 2006), 201.

9. Thomas Friedman, *The Lexus and the Olive Tree: Understanding Globalization* (New York: Farrar, Straus and Giroux, 1999), 100.

10. Greg Walton, *China's Golden Shield: Corporations and the Development of Surveillance Technology in the People's Republic of China* (Montreal: Rights and Democracy, 2001), 5.

11. Chen Shui-bian, address at the London School of Economics, December 6, 1999.

Chapter 13. Corporate Redesign and the Business of Knowledge

Epigraph: Jerry Hirshberg, *The Creative Priority* (New York: HarperPaperbacks, 1999).

1. Friedrich von Hayek, "The Use of Knowledge in Society," *American Economic Review* (September 1945), 519–30. See also Peter F. Drucker, *Landmarks of Tomorrow* (New York: Harper, 1959), for the origin of the idea of "knowledge workers."

2. Michael Polanyi, *The Tacit Dimension* (Garden City, NY: Doubleday, 1966).

3. Lotus, *New Yorker,* March 6, 2000, 3.

Chapter 14. Designing Time

1. The Isocratic oration is named after the Greek orator Isocrates (436–338 BC).

Chapter 15. The Design of Private Knowledge

1. Judith Herman, *Trauma and Recovery* (New York: Basic Books, 1992), 177 ff.

2. Jim Dwyer and Kevin Flynn, *102 Minutes: The Untold Story of the Fight to Survive Inside the Twin Towers* (New York: Times Books, 2005), 261.

3. On this discussion, see "The Science and Politics of Recovered Memory," *Ethics and Behavior,* 8, no. 2 (1998).

Acknowledgments

For their generosity and time in the course of this project, I wish to thank Michele Rubin, William Frucht, Mary Pasti, Christina Tucker, Jerry Hirshberg, David Rothenberg, Charles Muscatine, Richard Bender, John Parman, Eric Labrecque, Matt Taylor, Gail Taylor, Todd Johnston, Hélène Golay, Ray Sherman, Jack Shoemaker, Tom Allen (in memoriam), David McKinley, Julia Bolton Holloway, the Herman Miller Corporation, the Pinacoteca Nazionale of Siena, the Palazzo Te of Mantua, Churchill Heritage, and, as always, my wife, Michaela Paasche Grudin.

Index

Abramoff, Jack 144–45
Accademia del Disegno 86
Agrippa, Marcus 125
Alexander, Christopher 32
Al-Farabi 138
Al-Kindi 137–38
Allen, Tom 117
Alphonso the Wise 138
Anguissola, Sofonisba 93, 96–98, 100, 193
Anthony, Susan B. 142
Antoninus, Marcus Aurelius 81
Antony, Mark 125
Anxious class 70
Arcimboldo, Giuseppe 93
Aretino, Pietro 92
Aristotle 90, 107, 137–39
Athletics 168–70
Avempace 138
Averroes 138
Avicenna 138

Bacon, Francis 81, 108
Beauvoir, Simone de 142
Beethoven, Ludwig van 168
Bembo, Pietro 99, 101
Berruguete, Pedro 89–92, 96
Bibbiena, Bernardo 99
Bin Laden, Osama 44–45
Bisticci, Vespasiano da 90–91

Blake, William 131–33
Boccaccio, Giovanni 101, 138–40
Bouman, Ole 34
Bramante, Donato 15–16, 25
Breasted, Jim 11, 26
Bronzino, Agnolo 93
Bruegel, Pieter (the Elder) 93
Buber, Martin 58
Bush, George H. W. 144
Bush, George W. 106, 135, 144
Buffalmacco, Buonamico 63
Bull, Cornelius 185–86

Campi, Bernardino 96–98
Caesar, Augustus 125–28, 131, 133
Caligula 127
Carlson, Julius 73
Castiglione, Baldassare 98–102, 104, 194
Cellini, Benvenuto 93
Chandler, Raymond 22–23
Charles V 32, 93–95
Chen Shui-bian 147
Churchill, Winston 56–57, 108
Christo 19–20
Cicero, Marcus Tullius 100, 108, 118–19, 194–95
Citroën Deux Chevaux 12–13
Civility in design 22
Clement VII 92, 95
Clinton, Bill 144

Cohen, Roger 41
Comenius, Jan Amos 141
Common Cause 144
Conrad, Joseph 45
Cosimo I 86

Dante Alighieri 101, 138–39
Davenant, William 103
Da Vinci, Leonardo. *See* Leonardo da Vinci
Dean, James 69
De Gaulle, Charles 12
DeLay, Thomas D. (Tom) 144
Della Porta, Giacomo 16
De Mestral, George 105
Derrida, Jacques 20, 190
Design, designo, designare 85–86, 128
Dewey, John 142
Dobbs, Lou 144–45
Dollfuss, Engelbert 55–56
Donatello 141
Douglass, Frederick 142
Dreams as psychological designs 186–88
Dwyer, Jim 182

Eames, Charles 10, 193
Earl, Harley 67
Edsel 12–15
Edsel scale 52–54
Epictetus 81
Erasmus, Desiderius 141
Euclid 137

Farabi, Al- 138
Faye, Emmanuel 59–60
Feinstein, Dianne 144
Filler, Martin 42
Flynn, Kevin 182
Ford Edsel 12–15
Foucault, Michel 190
Frank, Barney 144
Franklin, Benjamin 62, 108, 129
Frederick II 138
Freemasons 128–29
Fregoso, Ottaviano 99

French Revolutionary calendar 81
Freud, Sigmund 186–87
Friedman, Thomas 146
Fritsche, Johannes 58–59

Galen 137
Galsworthy, John 22
Gates (Christo and Jeanne-Claude) 20
Gehry, Frank 20–21
Gershwin, Ira 192
Gibbons, Gillian 40
Gilbert, Cass 42
Goethe, J. W. von 109
Gombrich, Ernst 100
Gonzaga, Elisabetta 99
Gonzaga, Federico 6, 93, 95, 99
Google 162–65
Grabar, Oleg 39–40
Graham, Paul 33, 46
Greco, El 93
Greenspan, Alan 154
Gropius, Walter 56

Hall of the People 18
Haydn, Joseph 102, 167
Hayek, Friedrich von 123, 155–56
Hayward, Marta (pseudonym) 52–54
Hegel, G. W. F. 45
Heidegger, Martin 58–60
Herman, Judith 180–81, 186
Heskett, John 23
Hideyoshi. *See* Toyotomi Hideyoshi
Hippocrates 137
Hirshberg, Jerry 68, 150
Hitler, Adolf 18, 55–60
Homer 88–89
Hood, Raymond 42
Hopwood, Bert 24
Horace 32
Hughes, Robert 42
Humanism as a knowledge design 31, 40–41, 90–92, 103, 107–10, 137, 139–42, 165
Hussein, Saddam 135
Husserl, Edmund 58
Huxtable, Ada Louise 42

Ibn Khaldun 138
Intentional days 111–16, 175–77
Isocrates 171–72

Jaffe, Lee 36, 45
James, William 142
Jefferson, Thomas 51–52, 62, 90, 107–12,
    117–21, 129, 131, 133–36, 140, 142, 150,
    194
Jesus 108
Johnson, Lyndon 142
Johnson, Philip 43
Johnston, Todd 122
Jones, Inigo 32

Kern, Jerome 192
Kerr, Laurie 39–40
Khalife, Marcel 40
Khomeni, Ayatolla 136
Kindi, Al- 137–38
King, Martin Luther, Jr. 142
Klee, Paul 56
Knights Templar 128
Knowledge designs 7, 31, 79–82, 89–92,
    99, 134–43, 150–65, 178–92
K Street 144–45

La Boétie, Étienne de 141
Latini, Brunetto 138–40, 150
Lehár, Franz 184
Leonardo da Vinci 85–86
Liberty 7, 57, 61, 62, 64, 95, 110, 120, 122,
    124, 134–49, 194–95
Lincoln, Abraham 142
Locke, John 108
Lubitsch, Ernst 185
Luxemburg, Rosa 55

MacDonald, Jeanette 184–85
Machiavelli, Niccolò 101–2, 110–11, 115,
    140, 141
Maderno, Carlo 16, 17, 193
Mamun 137
Mannerism 93–104
Mansfield, Harvey 124
Marcus Aurelius 81

May, Rollo 123
McKinley, William 124
McNamara, Robert 14
McQueen, Steve 69
Medici, Giuliano de' 99
Memory as a psychological
    design 184–86
Michelangelo 15–16, 25, 93, 96
Mies van der Rohe, Ludwig 42–43, 56
Milton, John 141
Montaigne, Michel de 102, 141
Montefeltro, Federico da 89–90, 193
Montefeltro, Guidobaldo da 99
Monteverdi, Claudio 32, 102–4
Morris, Langdon 121
Morris, William 129–30
Mozart, Wolfgang Amadeus 102–3
Muir, John 142

Narrative as a psychological
    design 178–86
National Gallery of Art 19
Nazism and design 17–18, 55–61
Nero 127
Nerva 127
Newman, Paul 69
Newton, Isaac 108
Norman, Donald 46
Norton Dominator 11–12, 21–22, 24–25,
    193

Obama, Barack 148–49
Orwell, George 77
Overdesign 14–18, 25

Palazzo Te 6, 32, 93–96, 98
Parmenides 156
Parsons, Frank Alvah 130
Patton, George 50
Pei, I. M. 19
Perugino, Pietro 93
Peterson, Merrill 117
Philip II 96
Plato 107, 137, 156
Polanyi, Michael 156
Popper, Karl 58

Ptolemy 137
Public policy 15–18

Qutb, Sayyid 44

Raimondi, Marcantonio 92
Rand, Ayn 154
Raphael 93
Raskin, Jef 22, 53
Rathenau, Walther 55
RCA Building 42
Rhetoric 15–21, 32, 42–43, 44, 118, 136,
   171–75
Rikyu, Sen no 3–4, 34, 45, 55, 60–62,
   86–87, 99
Rockefeller, David 35, 45
Robertson, Leslie 38
Rogers, Carl 123
Röhm, Ernst 55–56
Romano, Giulio 6, 32, 92–96, 97–98,
   102, 104, 129
Roosevelt, Franklin Delano 124
Roosevelt, Theodore 124, 131, 133, 144
Rousseau, Jean-Jacques 62
Rower, Howard 12
Rudolf II 32

Salutati, Coluccio 139
Schama, Simon 88
Schleicher, Kurt von 55
Schmitt, Carl 59
Schopenhauer, Arthur 166
Seagram Building 43
Self-design 105–15
Sen no Rikyu. See Rikyu, Sen no
Serra, Richard 19
Shakespeare, William 97–98, 102, 103,
   167–68, 170, 172–73, 176, 179–80,
   189–90
Shaw, George Bernard 150
Simon, Herbert 3
Socrates 106–7
Sottsass, Ettore 10
Speer, Albert 17–18
Sprezzatura 100
Spinoza, Benedict (or Baruch) 141

Stata Center 20–21
St. Peter's Basilica 15–17, 25, 193
Stumpf, Bill 22, 193
Subjectivity as a psychological
   design 188–91
Sullivan, Louis 14, 43

Tanks 50–51
Taylor, Matt 24, 122–23
Tea ceremony 3–4, 60–61
Tilted Arc (Serra) 19
Tocqueville, Alexis de 135
Toyotomi Hideyoshi 3–4, 28, 59–61
Tozzoli, Guy 36, 45
Trauma therapy 178–81, 186
Truth in design 10–33, 43, 62, 64, 79–82,
   95, 115–16, 143, 153, 175, 180, 187, 192,
   193–95

Uthman, Wail 44

Van de Velde, Henri 130
Vasari, Giorgio 85–87, 93–94, 96, 129,
   131, 141
Velcro 78, 105
Verdi, Giuseppe 104
Von Oech, Roger 191
Voravetvuthikun, Sirivat 146

Wagner, Richard 104
Wagner, Robert F. 35
Wankel, Felix 164
Washington, George 134
Weil, Simone 81
Whitman, Walt 142
Williams, Roger 141
William the Silent 141
Wittgenstein, Ludwig 58
Woolworth Building 42
World Trade Center 35–45, 48
Wright, Frank Lloyd 24, 123, 177

Yamasaki, Minoru 6, 34–45, 183